The Radio and Television Commercial

Instructions for Page Removal

The pages of this book have been perforated so that the user may remove them easily. To remove any page, simply follow these steps:

1. Hold backbone of book in left hand.
2. With right thumb and index finger grasp page to be removed about two inches from the top of page.
3. With thumb and index finger pull page down and away from the spine (backbone).
4. Use a steady pull rather than ripping suddenly.

The Radio and Television Commercial

ALBERT C. BOOK

Professor of Journalism
School of Journalism, University of Nebraska

NORMAN D. CARY

Senior Associate Professor, Mass Media
Bucks County Community College

Crain Books
A Division of Crain Communications Inc.
740 Rush Street
Chicago, Illinois 60611

International Standard Book Number: 0-87251-038-7
Library of Congress Classification: LC 78-529597

Portions of this book have previously been published as parts of *The Television Commercial: Creativity and Craftsmanship*, by Albert C. Book and Norman D. Cary, copyright © 1970 by Crain Communications Inc.

Printed in the United States of America.

Second printing, 1980.

Design and typesetting: North Coast Associates.

Contents

Preface

Like most businesses, advertising combines science and fact with art and creativity. Science and fact can be absorbed, reflected upon, and utilized, while art and creativity can be encouraged, guided and developed. Our primary purpose in this book is to help develop the art of creating effective radio and television advertising.

In this book, we hope to reach and direct the individual who may be preparing for a career in advertising, marketing, or associated areas in industry. To do this, we analyze the techniques of current radio and television commercial structures and offer practical guides toward producing and judging well designed sales messages in these media.

Millions of dollars of advertisers' money are wasted each year because commercials are carelessly designed, poorly written, and amateurishly produced. This book, perhaps serving as a background for a copywriter, producer, art director, agency account executive, or advertising manager, can help reduce the number of such failures.

Some day in the future, you may help create commercials while working for an ad agency, or you may sit in judgment on them as a client. Right now, we look at you as a person with ideas. We hope the ideas will be fresh and original. With a developed sense of form and craftsmanship, you can incorporate these ideas into commercials which will be noticed and acted upon.

A creator of radio and television commercials must work within current broadcast standards and also answer to his own conscience in matters of honesty, taste, and discretion. How he accepts this responsibility is vital to his success as an advertising practitioner and is just as vital to his sense of personal integrity.

A. B.
N. C.

Section I
Broadcast Advertising

Chapter 1
Creativity and Craftsmanship

What makes a commercial an effective sales tool? Basically, it's usually the result of an intriguing idea placed in a unified structure and developed with creativity, ingenuity, and insight. The structure may be one of many, or a combination. The sell may be direct, even "hard," or it may be suggestive, seductive, and "soft," as long as it offers a benefit to which a viewer or listener can relate and react.

Viewer response to radio and television

A prospect responds far differently to broadcast media than he does to advertisements in print. A newspaper or magazine ad can be totally ignored, quickly scanned, or thoroughly read. The time devoted to each message depends upon the interest aroused and developed in the product or idea. Television and radio commercials interrupt programming content as a print advertisement interrupts the editorial content of a magazine or newspaper, but the audio and audio/visual commercials are more obtrusive, more abrupt, more jarring. They must run out their time span. No wonder, then, that the public's responses to these spots are more vocal—and more varied.

While most listeners and viewers accept the fact that commercials are the price they must pay for "free" television and radio, many low opinions of broadcast ads are heard in coffee-klatch and office-break conversations. According to a study by Elmo Roper and Associates, the public's attitude is more favorable than hostile toward TV commercials, but the number who actively dislike them is substantial. More recent consumer attitudes, as reported by a leading advertising agency, are reflected in such comments as these in the consumer press:

> . . . commercials are way ahead of most TV programs in being tuned to the 'big beat' to which America pulses.

> They are an American art form. A minor art form but the ultimate in mixed media: sight, sound and sell.

A distinction should be drawn between TV and radio commercials. It is easier for a listener to close an ear to a radio spot than it is to close eyes and ears to a TV sales message. People usually have stronger likes and dislikes for TV spots, whereas they tend not to develop forceful stands on radio commercials. There have been countless examples of spots that were irritating and intruding but yet sold the product, at least for a while. Love-hate relationships aside, the key is to get the prospect to stop, look, listen, be persuaded—and act.

Behind the criticism

In order to create broadcast media sales messages that work, the questions should be asked, "Why are viewers so critical of TV advertising?" and "Why are listeners so docile about radio spots?" There are many answers, but first and foremost is the nature of each medium. Television combines sight, color, voice, music, movement, sound, and visual effects. It is difficult to ignore such a potent combination of attention-getting elements. For its part, radio offers an involving mixture of voice, music, sound effects, *and,* importantly, unbridled use of imagination. For both radio and TV there is no page to be turned; they must be allowed their allotted seconds.

As a result, the time span of commercials, whether ten seconds or two minutes, is an insistent presence. Even if someone looks away from the television screen, or steps out of the room, the audio portion can still be heard. If the message is presented in an interesting structure, with imaginative use of technique, if it captures attention, holds interest, creates desire, then it should succeed.

The question must be asked why so many commercials arouse criticism or, worse, fail to intrigue the listener/viewer and be all but totally ignored. There are, of course, many answers, but two keep recurring in research. First, many copywriters take for granted that the name of the product or service will be remembered even though experts have insisted that almost two-thirds of all commercials fail to register the name. Second, the construction of many commercials is haphazard to the point of weakness—the dreary sameness and irksome cliches, the exaggeration, and strident overclaiming. These practices show disregard for the taste and sensitivity of the viewer, insult his intelligence, and arouse resentment or generate apathy.

About 50,000 TV commercials are produced in the United States each year. The number of radio commercials is all but incalculable. Since TV viewing and radio listening vary, it is difficult to approximate norms of exposure to commercials. But it has been estimated that a young adult might hear 2,500 radio spots each month and view about 1,000 TV spots. Only a haldful of these can be considered to be outstanding selling vehicles. Fewer win awards.

Evidence of the combined skills of creative craftsmen is found among the award winners of a number of annual competitions, both regional and national. The winners of the gold statuette Clio awards (presented annually by the American Television and Radio Commercials Festival) enter the pantheon. In nearly every case the key ingredient is that much-used, often abused word "creativity." Certain advertising professionals decry the proliferation of awards, claiming that much of the judging concentrates on techniques and/or humorous approaches rather than on sales effectiveness to determine the winners.

This point is well-taken. Some commercials, although award winners in competition, have been abject failures in producing sales. Other commercials, not even allowed entrance into competitions, have helped create dramatic rises in sales curves. It is therefore obvious that there is no single path to effectiveness, but there can be guideposts along the way. And the immediate guideposts point to the idea and the structure used to convey it as being the most important aspects of the commercial.

Where do ideas come from?

The distinguished writer, John Steinbeck, in *East of Eden* (Viking Press, 1952), wrote: "Our species is the only creative species, and it has only one creative instrument: the individual mind and spirit of man. Nothing was ever created by two men. There are no good collaborations, whether in music, in art, in poetry, in mathematics, in philosophy. Once the miracle of creation has taken place, the group can develop it, but the group never invents anything."

Taken in its purest sense, this is true. Ideas do begin "in the lonely mind of a man." In any commercial, the *idea* is the spark that, fanned into flame by keen craftsmanship, lifts the commercial above mediocrity and achieves something distinctive, memorable, and effective. Without a strong central idea a commercial is likely to be dull, prosaic, imitative—and ineffective.

How do ideas begin to take form? Psychologists from William James on have explored the question. Dr. Gary Steiner narrows the search to commercials in *The People Look at Television* (Alfred A. Knopf, 1963). "Every creative idea," he says, "is initially a departure from present ways of doing things." Writers depart from an accepted, workable base because times change, attitudes change, taste and fashions change. And these things change all the more quickly in a society that has a high degree of mobility and a vast quantity of communications. Each change brings with it a new problem or set of problems. So, in the business of marketing and selling, in the use of advertising, new solutions must be found to new problems. And this demands thinking in new ways and combinations.

Dr. Steiner defines creativity as "the ability to produce and implement new and better solutions to any kind of a problem—to the writing of the copy, to the problem of deciding where and when to advertise, to the problem of how to organize a company." A copywriter's ability is always challenged to "produce and implement new and better solutions" but especially so when pressured by time, budget, and competitive limitations.

Your ally—creativity

While poets create to enlighten and composers to entertain, advertising writers create to change minds and alter buying decisions. This function of creativity should be kept constantly in mind. William Bernbach of Doyle, Dane, Bernbach summed it up when reporting on the planning of an important campaign: "We had neither the time nor the money to impress our message through sheer weight and repetition. We had to call in our ally—creativity. We had to startle people into an immediate awareness of our advantages in such a way that they would never forget it."

The effectiveness of creativity applied to an advertising problem for radio or TV is, therefore, not only the abstract of an idea but also the concrete consequence of that idea presented in such a way that it will arrest attention, startle an awareness, arouse a desire, and help effect a buying decision. Just as a successful salesman carefully plans an in-person call from entering an office to closing the order, so too must a copywriter work within some kind of form or structure. The advantages, especially for a beginning copywriter, of using a sound structure are evident: it helps alert and carry the listener/viewer along the time span of the sales message and serves as a vehicle for the ideas that change minds or reinforce current buying habits. It can be concluded that effective commercials call for imaginative creativity and careful craftsmanship.

Chapter 2
The Selling Idea

No advertisement should exist without a selling idea. Certainly no radio or television commercial is effective without one. No matter what structure or technique the commercial uses, the selling idea is the motivational force that changes consumer minds.

Selling is as old and practiced as man's recorded history. Ancient businessmen of Ephesus and Pompeii carved sales messages in stone. Early bazaars displayed goods, and merchants extolled the products with voice and gesture. Street vendors in old England developed special cries and songs for their cakes or fruit or flowers. Inns and taverns, long before most people could even read or had access to newspapers, advertised themselves with signs that indicated their business. Barber poles and pawnbroker symbols still exist to serve as instantly recognizable reminders of the specific business idea.

Not until the eighteenth century, when printing expanded and literacy increased, did advertising notices appear in print. Magazines, with their eventual development of high-quality color reproduction, greatly aided the beginnings of mass marketing. It remained for radio, with its imaginative use of sound, music, and words, and for television, with its addition of sight and motion, to take full advantage of mass communications for sales persuasion.

With so much working for you on radio and TV it might appear easy to overemphasize technique (and underemphasize the importance of the selling idea) and let the medium do your job. Don't fall into this deceptive trap. Each commercial must have a selling idea (or theme or sales proposition), the vital component of persuasion. The idea should come before the technique or structure.

A selling idea may appear suddenly, miraculously, but don't count on it. In most instances it must be planned for and cultivated. You should start with facts, product and prospect research. Then you work toward the goal of a provocative, imaginative, and cogent persuasive idea to be expressed in a memorable phrase. How? There are almost as many systems for working as there are copywriters.

Almost every sound method, however, begins with the basic human needs and wants. In their simplest forms, five of the most basic are shelter, food, clothing, appreciation (a sense of love), and vanity. Psychologist William James drew up a list of more than a hundred motivations that trigger response and action. Of course, not all humans have identical combinations of needs, or writing advertising that sells might be easier. But most people do worry or feel a lack in their lives if these basic needs or their variety of wants are not filled.

If your product or service fills one or a combination of these needs and does it better than competition, then you have found the psychological foundation for your selling campaign.

Using the procedures in the following checklist may help you build your advertising plan efficiently.

1. Research

a. Know your customers and prospects. Who buys your kind of product. Who uses your service. Where. How often. Why. Put yourself in your customer's shoes. Get to know what need might trigger a desire for your product. Is the need emotional. Is the want practical. Again, ask many questions in your consumer research.

b. Know your product (or service). Inside and out. What it is. How it's made. What needs it answers. How. What makes it better than competition. Any special ingredients. Method of manufacture. Competent product research should elicit dozens of questions. Be sure to get specific answers.

c. Know your competition. What other products or services similar to yours are available. How are they made. What features are better or worse than those of your product. How. Why. Are they virtually similar, like many cigarettes, beer, and gasolines. Your market and advertising research should explore their selling themes and performance claims. Does competition have a genuine, demonstrable advantage, or is it a performance characteristic that the advertiser has pre-empted.

2. The copy platform

When you are satisfied that you know who your customers are, what needs your product satisfies, and how your product compares with competition, you may feel somewhat overwhelmed. But having these facts is necessary to creation of a sound marketing plan and a clear-cut advertising strategy. In the process, decisions will have to be made about the role of radio and television advertising in the marketing effort. After positive decisions are made to use broadcast media, you can begin to develop copy platforms for radio and TV ads: objectives, audiences, prospect profiles (including attitudes about your product category), product advantages to be featured, and methods of presentation. Now you're ready to create spots.

3. Think it over

The genesis of an idea can be purely inspirational and can occur any time after you have absorbed background facts, but don't count on it. An enormous amount of concentrated thought can go into the development of a selling idea. Facts fed into your consciousness boil and turn. They are even affected by your subconscious. An idea for a bread commercial came to David Ogilvy and awoke him out of a sound sleep. He wrote it down and used it the next day to create an appealing TV spot. Of course, much conscious thought had already gone into solving the problem. It is a popular belief that there are no new ideas, only refreshing combinations of old ones, so don't overlook possible combinations or extensions in your thinking.

4. Talk it over

Once you have some ideas on paper, choose a friend or co-worker and try out your copy approaches. A fresh mind can often spot a weakness that you have failed to see. Better yet, by verbalizing your approach, you may find that you can more readily select and modify an idea, see it in a new light or at a unique angle.

5. If you hit a blank wall

Even experienced pros sometimes run into a dry spell. There are ways to get your thoughts going again if you seem to be stuck temporarily. These vary with individuals. Some sleep on the problem. Some take up another chore and return to the problem with fresh perspective. Others flail away at typewriter and drawing pad and put down dozens of thoughts, almost any thoughts, wild or tame, hopeful that one may lead to the selling idea.

Here is one helpful suggestion. Choose a friend and write him a letter (one you probably won't send). Make it sincere, persuasive, and, because he is your good friend, personal. Try to convince him of your product's advantages. Loosen your writing style, be your real self, communicate on a one-to-one basis. (Such a relationship, not so incidentally, is the basis of radio and TV selling: although your audience may number in the millions, you direct your appeal to one person at a time). As your letter develops you may discover yourself writing about the product in a different, new way. A gem of an idea may strike you and, figuratively, leap off the page.

6. Test, try, refine

When you feel confident that you have a solid, worthwhile selling idea, compare it with the selling themes of competitors. Be as objective as you can. Try it out on someone whose opinion you value. Check it against the marketing plan and advertising strategy. If it doesn't quite fit, work with variations of the idea. Move words around. Substitute. But always cast it in terms of your prospect's self-interest.

Words and sounds (and for television any possible visual treatment) are your basic materials, but the connotations and implied meanings of words are your allies. Just as outstanding chefs can give a special taste to a run-of-the-menu recipe, so too can an imaginative creator of TV or radio spots bring uniqueness to a selling theme. Words can shock, soothe, stimulate, agitate (even as these words evoke a response in you). Active words, words with vitality, can give your selling theme life of its own. Be sure that they communicate precisely and truthfully. Make them move your prospect to attention, agreement, acceptance—and action.

If your product's name can become part of the selling idea you are closer to success. Old Milwaukee Beer takes advantage of the fact that it is named for "the city that means beer." The makers of L'eggs stockings and pantyhose have combined a sophisticated mixture of name, product use, and an easily recognizable package. Avis gained ground on Hertz in car rentals by positioning itself as Number Two but vowing to "try harder." And 7-Up positioned itself as unique by calling itself the "Un-cola."

And don't overlook the mnemonic benefits of a distinctive sound. Again, the closer it can identify your product the more effectively it will work. Janitor-in-a-Drum not only gives the packaged appearance of a heavy-duty cleaner, but it also sounds like one when it is set down, barrel-like, on a floor.

7. Now let the commercial take shape

With a strong selling idea set within a memorable theme or phrase, you are ready to give it persuasive form as a radio or television commercial. An obvious next question involves what structure the commercial will take. While you may have had some thoughts about structure, form, or technique during the development process, there is danger in putting technique before the selling idea. Putting the commercial cart (structure) before the motivating horse (selling idea) often obstructs the way and impedes progress toward a fresh, new approach.

Above all, keep your selling idea easy to understand. Your theme or phrase may be as short as the successful "Coke—It's the real thing!" It may be as extended as the early Clairol line, "Does she or doesn't she? Only her hairdresser knows for sure."

In the cola example, Coca-Cola is fighting to enhance and extend its share of the market, is reaffirming its pre-eminence, originality, and "firstness" in the field. By saying that it is the "real thing" Coca-Cola seems to be inviting the prospect to infer that other colas are followers, perhaps not "real."

In the Clairol case, hair coloring was treated as a contemporary, natural-looking, entirely acceptable thing to do in a decade when this was only beginning to be true. Attractive young mothers were shown informally with their attractive young children. A female listener/viewer could conclude from the ads that she would neither look unnatural nor be subject to the raised eyebrow or a fall from social acceptance. Here the visual treatment reinforced the words. This one brand helped establish an entire market and paved the way for the many types and brands of hair-coloring products taken for granted today.

8. Last, not least

Include your product's name in the selling theme. In an effective cat food spot, cats ask for Meow Cat Food by name. In another spot, the phrase, "Bounty—the quicker picker-upper," gets both name and claims into its short selling line. Never forget that competition is tough and apt to get tougher. You must get listeners and viewers to recall the product name, remember what the product does, and know how it performs. A long-time TV expert, Harry McMahon, has estimated that up to two-thirds of all TV commercials fail to register the product by brand name. Keep this statistic in mind when you create a commercial.

As your commercial unfolds, the sales message should come through clearly. The appropriate structure should be there to support it, move it along, and give it a framework. If you find the structure draws attention to itself and obscures the product name, you're probably working with the wrong structure. Remember, you're selling a product, not the structure.

With an effective sales theme in a compatible structure, your commercial stands a better chance of attracting attention, involving the prospective customer emotionally and/or logically, developing a desire to try the product, and leading him to purchase with a final bid to act.

In creating and crafting, you are fortunate in that you have easy access to radio and television. By attentive listening and watching, you become more aware of different selling ideas and how they are presented. While doing this you should ask a number of questions—and answer them. Are the spots direct and clear? Are they obscure? Do they state benefits? Imply? Do they appeal to emotion or logic?

Questions such as these should be asked when you study the examples of radio and television commercials in the sections that follow. Note the variety of structures and how the selling ideas are used within them. Be alert to their ultimate simplicity, clarity, and strong name identification.

Section II
Radio Commercials

Chapter 3

Dimensions of Radio

In 1922, Herbert Hoover, thirty-first President of the United States who was then Secretary of Commerce and charged with responsibility for administering the Radio Act of 1912, said:

> We have witnessed in the last four or five months one of the most astounding things that has come under my observation . . . today over 600,000 persons possess wireless telephone receiving sets, whereas there were less than 50,000 such sets a year ago.*

Mr. Hoover would undoubtedly be even more astounded to know that today there are almost 400 million radios in the United States, and that more than 98 percent of all American homes have at least one.

In 1923 there were 573 radio stations in the country; today there are about 7,000 AM and/or FM stations. More than 95 percent of cars have radios that are tuned in about 70 percent of driving time. For transistor radio batteries alone, teenagers and adults spent more than $200 million in 1977. Far from dying when that phenomenal intruder, television, entered the scene, radio has taken on a prosperous life of its own.

Back in the 1950s after the first devastating impact of television subsided, radio transformed itself. It turned to more modest programming and to many small advertisers to make up the revenue it had lost. It began to feature what had been its filler material, using news and music as its staples and seeking sectional and local rather than national advertisers. Through foresight, flexibility, and innovation, radio has revitalized itself and become a prime medium for advertisers, large and small.

Today, large cities may have 20 or more radio stations, and even small country towns usually have an AM outlet. With such localizing of audiences, retailers have taken full advantage of radio as an advertising medium. That it works can be inferred from a Radio Advertising Bureau (RAB) survey which claims that local business more than doubled in the last decade. In the mid-1970s, radio advertising revenue exceeded $1 billion annually.

People listen to radio primarily for information, news, music, talk, entertainment, and sports. Nearly 95 percent of the population, twelve years of age and over, listens to some radio broadcasts every day. And from early morning to the start of prime evening time, more people listen to radio than watch television. Interestingly, the RAB reports that more than 50 percent of the adult population rate radio as a release from loneliness and boredom. This indicates that radio is a very personal, very acceptable, and very selective medium for advertisers.

Important, too, is the psychological fact that radio is an intimate, friendly medium. Disc jockeys, open mike hosts, and local commentators attract and hold their audiences today as did the network personalities of the "golden age" when *Fibber McGee and Molly, Amos 'n' Andy,* and Jack Benny were tune-in musts.

Radio early established an amazing believability. Orson Welles' dramatic 1938 broadcast "visualized" an invasion from Mars that had thousands of listeners fleeing their homes in terror. As Mr. Welles said at a radio workshop, "Oh, we knew that radio, used inventively, could glue the listener to his overstuffed Morris chair, get him involved and make him believe . . . but we never dreamed to what extent."

Acceptance, friendliness, and believability are aspects of radio that should not be ignored by anyone attempting to write effective commercials. Advertisers, large or local, wisely include radio in their media mix. Accounts with even modest national budgets can work wonders with radio alone. One jams and jellies company, Smucker, has used radio extensively with a unique creative approach to establish its name

---

* "Minutes of Open Meetings of Department of Commerce Conference on Radio Telephony," mimeographed (Washington, D.C.: Department of Commerce, 1922), p. 2.

nationally. Most supermarket brands sold for a few cents less than Smucker's, so radio spots had to give housewives the idea of high quality. This goal was accomplished with a mildly self-deprecatory "recall trap." (See Chapter 5, "Writing for Radio.") Every spot used this reminder: "With a name like Smucker's it has to be good." Listeners across the country could identify this line, could readily recall the brand name, and could play back the quality image.

Many other advertisers have picked radio and used it extensively, if not exclusively. General Mills, which found success with heavy spot radio campaigns for Nature Valley Granola and Granola Bars, Breakfast Squares, and Golden Grahams, has boosted its radio spending from zero to more than $2 million annually. Continental Airlines, smallest of the 10 major U.S. trunk airlines, invests $2 million in radio advertising annually. And Midas International, after adding radio to its usual TV schedule, credited that mix with boosting sales 30 percent.

It should be remembered, however, that such success is not automatic. People seldom just sit and listen attentively. They are busy doing other things while their radios are turned on. More, perhaps, than with any other advertising medium, the basics of attention, interest, involvement, and conviction must be achieved in each radio commercial.

Radio has also made great strides in audience measurement. Gone is the idea of *homes* listening to radio, for homes don't listen. People listen. The old technology did not keep up with the multiplicity of radio sets around the house, the car, and the office. The old mechanical gadgetry underestimated radio's audience. So the industry—the Radio Advertising Bureau and the National Association of Broadcasters combined—undertook the All-Radio Methodology Study (ARMS I) to determine which methods of audience measurement might truly reflect reality.

As a result, better ways of counting audience were developed. Advertisers on radio now have a much better idea of what their dollars deliver. Along with local market studies done by ARB, Pulse, Mediastat, Hooper, The Source, and others, a national measurement was developed. The national networks cooperated to develop their own study to replace the old Nielsen national homes-listening research based on meters too large to be attached to all the sets in a household.

Chapter 4

Advantages of Radio

Some media prophets of gloom and doom predicted radio's demise as an advertising medium when television entered the scene. They couldn't have been more wrong. Radio revenues did dip drastically, but broadcasters examined the medium for its strengths, fed and exercised them, and came up with new programming—and commercial health. Radio, today, is a potent selling tool for good reasons. These five stand out:

1. Radio is ubiquitous. Half a billion radios are in working order. Most of them are in homes from bedroom to kitchen, in stores, and in barbershops and offices. Trucks and cars account for well over 100 million of them. And portable radios by the scores of millions are toted just about everywhere— even to sporting events that are being broadcast play by play. (Perhaps television has conditioned some people to want to hear a running description of what they are seeing.)

2. Radio is selective. Geographic, demographic, and programming diversity of radio stations helps media buyers pinpoint their target audiences. Such flexibility means that your spots might be read by a live announcer on local stations. Or they could be broadcast on regional networks or on one stretching from coast to coast. Spots can be scheduled for as few or as many plays as objectives and budget dictate. They can be broadcast at just about any hour of the day or night. Advertisers can choose from a variety of AM or FM stations, each with a distinctive format: all news, top forty (popular music), beautiful music, middle of the road (MOR), classical, soul, ethnic, or foreign language. Such diversity allows the copywriter to "speak" directly to his intended prospects.

3. Radio is economical. In a single week radio reaches 9 out of 10 people twelve years of age and over. Those eighteen and older listen on an average of 3 hours and 22 minutes each day. An advertiser can usually count on an effective combination of reach and frequency for a relatively low cost per thousand listeners. Alone or in a mix with other media, radio can effectively help stretch ad budgets.

Another economy: radio commercials are comparatively inexpensive to produce, ranging from no-cost when a script or ad-lib fact sheet is used by a live/local announcer to a modestly budgeted full production with music, sound effects (SFX), and talent.

4. Radio is fast. If the need arises, an advertiser can have a live/local commercial on the air within hours. Spots using sound effects, music or jingle, and several voices can be rehearsed, recorded, mixed, dubbed, and be played on the air within days. This is a break for advertisers who must meet occasional emergencies, such as an air-conditioner dealer whose territory is suddenly smothered by a heat wave.

5. Radio is participatory. Along with a sense of friendliness and loyalty to a particular station, listeners develop a sense of involvement. Radio calls the imagination into play. There is virtually no restriction to locale. Sound effects and music instantly set a scene. Description or dialogue can be as vivid as taste allows, and characters can be played in any range from straight to extremely broad. The listener fills in the "color" and details with his imagination.

Any or all of the above characteristics of radio can be used by creative advertisers and agencies to prepare and present commercials that sell.

Creating and drafting radio commercials today is more difficult in some ways and easier in others than it was a generation ago. This seeming paradox, fortunately, has an explanation. Years ago techniques and mechanics were limited. Most commercials, both network and local, were performed live, with limited availability of music, sound effects, and talent. Recorded commercials were on discs and every element had to be performed, cued, and mixed as the master was cut. Today, the state of the art has advanced. Tape recording equipment and procedures can be virtually flawless. Multi-tracks are common, and microphones, mixing, and editing equipment are perfected. So today you have much more latitude in creativity and production which makes your job easier in the technical sense. But this wider choice of techniques makes your creative task more difficult.

Two other elements add to the difficulty of creating persuasive radio spots. First, advertising competition has burgeoned as radio stations have multiplied. It is tougher to gain and hold the listener's attention. Second, the radio listener has changed. Because of the growing number of ad impressions in all media, many people have consciously or unconsciously managed to block out unwanted sounds. Offensive, loud, jangly radio spots are considered to be noise pollutants.

Add to this the fact that people no longer sit quietly in living rooms listening to radio as they did in pre-television times. People listen to radio in just about any room in their homes. Most of the time you're fighting for their attention. Their ears are not riveted to the radio. A housewife may be preparing dinner, ironing, trying to get the kids off to school, or perhaps just talking with a neighbor. Your commercial may come on as a driver weaves through traffic, a vacationist suns on the beach, a patient waits in a dentist's office, a farmer feeds his cattle, a man shaves, or a couple parks in some secluded nook. Unlike your TV audience, a radio audience might be anywhere, its attention could be divided.

This means more competition for attention.

It also means that a radio commercial must have a solid selling idea presented in an attention-getting way. Above all, you must break the barrier of boredom. As old-pro Charlie Brower of BBDO said, "The cardinal sin in advertising is to be dull."

Most copywriters happily accept this challenge. Warren Pfaff, a senior vice-president of J. Walter Thompson says:

> If you want to be a good writer, think about radio first. Radio's the little box without eyes, and it doesn't give you an art director to lean on; it doesn't give you any socko picture to bail you out. You're all alone with the listener and somehow you've got to hit him between the eyes even when his eyes are closed. Once you've learned to do that, you've just got to be a better writer. In any medium.

Where to start

You begin with a selling idea, a unique selling proposition, a distinct product advantage in a memorable phrase. Add a relevant sound effect, or set the phrase to a musical figure, and you are ready for the next step—selecting your back-up appeal, your supporting sell. This may be emotional or logical, stated or implied. Or it might be a combination (as in some spots for sugarless gum). As stated in Chapter 2, "The Selling Idea," your approach must meet your advertising objectives (introduce a new product, revitalize an old one, give your product a new position against competition, etc.). Such decisions are not capricious; they are based on—it bears repeating—knowing your customer or prospect, knowing your product or service, and knowing the marketing situation (your competitors' strengths and weaknesses).

Multi-media use

If a campaign is to get exposure on television and radio, it is possible that the sound track of the TV spot can work for radio as well. But it should not be an after-thought, it must be pre-planned, written, and so produced. This is often the case when a jingle is the vehicle or technique employed to carry the sales message. Ads for soft drinks, beer, and even cars have successfully been made to do this, following the accepted media law of repetition and reminder.

Commercial formats for radio

As with TV commercials, there is no formula for success; otherwise a computer could create advertising. Generally, however, radio spots can be categorized according to the prominent techniques they use. Basically, radio ads fit into two groups.

1. Live announcement
   a. Announcer as spokesperson reads prepared script.
   b. Announcer as spokesperson refers to fact sheet of product information but ad-libs and extemporizes.
   c. A combination of spokesperson(s) and/or sound effects and/or music.
2. Recorded announcement
   a. Announcer as spokesperson reads prepared script while it is taped.
   b. Announcer as spokesperson ad-libs commercial based on product data in prepared fact sheet.
   c. A combination of talent, sound effects and/or music is recorded on tape(s); this recording is sometimes dubbed onto acetate discs.

Approaches should be keyed to objectives

You may wish to use the news or information approach to introduce a new product or to announce a store sale. You might use a jingle to promote brand loyalty in a very competitive market. You might sponsor opera performances or other cultural events to enhance your corporation's image.

By no means is this a complete list since the thousands of consumer products and services offered for sale differ in manufacture, versatility, and convenience. It is mandatory, however, that your radio strategy or approach be designed to meet your advertising objectives. With your creative foot on this step you are prepared to take the next one: write the commercial in a format compatible with your objectives and strategy, and with a technique that will emphasize the product rather than draw attention to itself.

Formats

The danger in setting down classifications of commercials by structure and technique is that it seems to codify creativity and limit experimentation. So this disclaimer is being made immediately: the following list is by no means limiting; these are com-

monly accepted terms well-known by professional copywriters. And they are well-used, individually and in combination. One writer claimed that there were 33 varieties of radio spots, but the ones listed here are heard most often:

1. Story line. A narrative development with a beginning, a developmental middle section, and a conclusion. To be effective, the story should concern the listener, should deal with his problems, and should offer a reward for listening.

2. Problem-solution. Perhaps the most popular structure since it opens with a listener-oriented problem and presents the product as the ever-handy solution. Must have some plausible basis in real life (or strong implication) to be accepted and believed.

3. Testimonial. A technique in which the selling message is given by the person or persons who benefitted directly from using the product or service. There should always be some legitimate basis for using a particular person as testifier to maintain believability. If you use a celebrity he must have used the product. This technique can take many forms—story line, problem-solution, spokesman, etc.

4. Spokesman. Or spokesperson. Usually a staff announcer of the radio station who reads the commercial script or ad-libs after referring to a fact sheet of product information. The writing style should fit the delivery style of the spokesman, whether hard-hitting and strong or more personal and intimate.

5. Demonstration. A difficult feat for radio, but possible if your demo has distinctive sounds or can be dramatically described. An alternative sometimes used is the wildly far-out demonstration that obviously exaggerates and at the same time entertains.

6. Suspense. Seldom used in radio because of the listener's short attention span plus the violation of the first law of radio commercials to get the product name in early and often. Suspense can be used as an element of other formats, but don't count on being able to use suspense by itself as a radio ad format.

7. Slice of life. Dramatic situations are the bread and butter of radio commercials. Dialogue between family members, friends, and neighbors remains a potent means for relating your product's benefits in an everyday, believable context. The style may be down to earth honest, mildly funny, or outrageously hilarious. As a technique it is often combined with a problem-solution structure.

8. Analogy. If a product or its attributes can easily be compared to some thing or action instantly familiar, then analogy is an interesting structure to attempt. But it is fraught with difficulties. The "just as . . . so too" comparison means that product benefits must be inferred by the listener, so make your point very clear.

9. Fantasy. This is a favorite of radio writers and listeners since it exercises vivid imagination in both groups. Obviously, it needs other formats (story line, slice of life, etc.) to give it structure. Use of fantasy can be highly entertaining, but great care must be taken in writing and production to ensure registration of the product benefits and listener rewards.

10. Personality. In radio spots this can mean the use of a celebrity or an actor/announcer with a distinctive vocal timbre or delivery. The key to success with this technique is to develop a strong character who is easily recognizable on repeat hearing and can generate empathy from listeners. Heard and accepted as an authority figure, the personality's dialogue may be written straight, with humor, or in a situation where the product benefits seem to be told conversationally.

11. Jingles. From their inception in the 1920s, words and music extolling a product or service have proven to be strong selling vehicles on radio. Rhythm and rhyme cloak the selling "medicine" with "sugar." An ad using this device, when well-written, is not only entertaining and pleasant, but it also becomes an instant memory trap, a reminder. Include the product name and repeat it. Keep the jingle length under 15 seconds—and repeat the entire jingle if it's a 60-second spot. For maximum recall, keep the music and lyrics simple.

Overlapping or combining structures is common practice, and the above-named categories are not intended to be mutually exclusive. For example, a testimonial might be straight, done dramatically in problem-solution or slice-of-life format, or presented as a fantasy. Give your creativity flexibility as well as form. Experiment first with individual structures, then develop combinations of approaches.

Commercial appeals

Technique alone doesn't make a commercial successful. Your spot must appeal to logic or the emotions. In Chapter 2, "The Selling Idea," several psychological appeals are discussed. If the structure or format can be considered the vehicle, then the appeal can be thought of as the fuel, the energy that makes your vehicle move.

If your product outperforms those of your competition there must be a reason. The sheer logic of fact might persuade a prospect. If your product has parity of performance with your competitors' products, you must find the inherent advantage that can be translated into a dramatic sensory, emotional or security appeal. Health, safety, sex, home, love, and sentiment are strong personal concerns, and ads for products with benefits in these areas should utilize appropriate appeals.

Status, whether individual, family, or group, evolves from ego—one of the strongest possible appeals. Almost everyone wants to look better, be more comfortable, and be appreciated. From your research (customer, product, competition) you'll find yourself thinking about feasible appeals.

Humor in commercials

Humor is a very popular technique with writers of radio spots, but not all ads using humor are effective. In fact, very few of them are genuinely funny. Humor is a favorite with beginning copywriters perhaps because it seems easy to write, a pleasant but often defeating deception. Real humor is exceedingly difficult to apply to sales messages. Too many radio writers think of themselves as budding Stan Frebergs, but unless the funny flair sounds Woody Allen spontaneous or George Carlin original you run the risk of eliciting groans instead of smiles, and cash registers will ring up "No Sale."

Even spots that titillate on first or second hearing may wear out their welcome quickly. (Who listens to and responds to the same joke after half a dozen hearings?) It is wiser to make your spot's situation or character funny or amusing by writing it pleasantly in an engaging style, making certain that the technique doesn't overshadow the sales message.

When producing a humorous spot, cast the voices and direct the tempo with careful regard for timing and inflection. Humor should never sound forced. To succeed it must be fresh and light.

Imagination—radio's big plus

Imaginations—the writer's and the listener's—work more effectively in radio advertising than in any other medium. The input is all audio: sound effects, voices, and music. You, as writer, are your own art director and are not bounded by print limitations or TV linearity. You create mental pictures and activate the imagination of your listeners. With attention riveted, interest increases, product points gain emphasis, and your spot is on its way to achieving its persuasive function.

You not only design and set the scene, you also can change time and scenery with your kit of audio tools. In seconds you can get the listener to picture a caveman in prehistory or a Martian in 2001.

As an example of the key role of imagination in radio copy, consider one of Stan Freberg's spots in which an "on-the-scene" announcer excitedly describes a thousand airplanes flying over Lake Michigan and dropping tons of cherries onto a frothy mountain of whipped cream. Imagination unlimited!

Another of radio's most inventive (and award-winning) copywriters, Chuck Blore, claims that there is nothing that cannot be done on radio "visually," using imagination. Larry Rood, who suggested the idea that the Mazda goes "Hummmmmmmm," believes that "Radio is the most visual of all media. You can create characters, situations, whole worlds that can't be duplicated in TV or print. When you create this imaginative situation, the listener can project himself into that world through imagination."

The operative words are "project himself." Your commercial must trigger your listener's imagination, participation, and involvement. Unless your commercial succeeds in this, it won't succeed in meeting its marketing and advertising goals.

Chapter 6
Radio Commercial Guidelines

Distilled from reviewing the successes and failures of radio advertising is the following list of do's and don't's. Consider these suggestions in deciding what will work best for your radio spot.

1. Capture and excite the listener's imagination.

By using sound only, your commercial performs in the "theater of the mind." With the competition your product (and commercial) faces, radio is no place to be dull, pedantic, or prosaic.

2. Stick to one strong idea.

Concentrate on communicating one *main* persuasive thrust. An extra copy point or two, woven into the continuity of the spot, can be used, but with care. Too many copy points confuse. Also, don't sell generically for the whole product category, sell *your* product's benefits.

3. Single out your prospect.

If you've done your research you know who buys your product and why. Keep your target consumer in mind when you write your commercials. If your product alleviates backache don't start by describing June roses. Get right to the point—"If you suffer the agony of a sore back. . . ." Your talent selection can help: a company making skin care products features Wolfman Jack talking to teenagers about acne in radio spots. Because of his involvement with popular music, he's a listened-to authority figure.

4. Set the mood for your product.

How fast should your commercial be delivered? What tone of voice should your "housewife" employ? Is the music too "busy" for your product's image? These and a dozen other questions come to mind when you write a commercial. Your answers will determine the "tone" or approach. To get the right one, you must be conscious of *how* you want the listener to hear—and react.

After deciding what tone you want, write

directions in your script as to how you wish a line to be read (*angry, sad, happy, irritated,* etc.). A spokesperson picking up your script should have specific directions. When you add your description of the kind of delivery you want, everyone from the client to the director is assisted.

It bears repeating: radio can do just about anything from an Honest John approach to fantastic satirical camp. Of course you must match the commercial tone to your product's image; they should be compatible. A wildly exaggerated dramatization wouldn't do for a Rolls Royce but it might be just perfect for a kid's cereal.

5. Remember your mnemonics.

Be sure to set a memory trap—and spring it. It might be copy, music, sound effects, or a combination thereof, but it must be meaningful. For example, if you were to be asked what kind of car goes "Hummmmmmm!" and what soup is "Mmmm-Mmmmgood!" chances are you'd answer Mazda and Campbell.

Diet Pepsi zips up a zipper and Parks Sausages have an insistent boy's voice pleading, "More Parks Sausages, Mom . . . please."

6. The first few seconds will make or break.

Your first chore is to get attention. The first five or six seconds are vital ones. If you fail here the whole spot may be wasted effort.

An automotive product begins a spot with an announcer (on filter, as if at a race oval) over a public address system: "Gentlemen, start your engines!" And shortly a roar of motors is heard. Expend a lot of creative thought on your opening.

7. Register the product name.

Some copy chiefs might add, "Early and often!" Since you don't have the big type of print advertising, you must establish the product or service name—and repeat it during the spot.

One commercial for Triumph cars begins with a local announcer giving a dealer's name and address followed by "... your Triumph dealer takes you out on the range." The pre-taped spot is cued with sound effects of a horse neighing and a Triumph TR-3 driving up and stopping. A cowboy drawls, "See you hitched up to a Triumph TR-3, Slim."

A listener can't help but identify the product name—and quickly.

Another device, so frequently used that it is becoming a cliche, involves spelling the product name. Kraft does this to help people remember how to spell cheese. Fotomat Stores use a humorous, fast-moving dramatization. (See Chapter 7.)

8. Don't overwrite.

Don't crowd your spot with too many words. Use easy-to-understand words, keep phrases and sentences on the short side. Write in the present tense, active voice as much as possible.

Read your commercial aloud, or have someone read it to you. Change any words which are difficult to pronounce or hinder smooth continuity. Allow for announcer breathing (and listener hearing) time. Word count varies with approaches, delivery, mood, etc., but the following is the recognized and generally accepted average for straight announcements:

  10 seconds: 20-25 words
  20 seconds: 40-45 words
  30 seconds: 60-70 words
  60 seconds: 150-180 words

9. Make your appeal clear.

There are five basic needs of man (shelter, food, clothing, appreciation or love, and vanity), but the wants of man seem unlimited. So you have a wide choice when it comes to selecting and crafting a persuasive appeal. A good question to ask is: "What basic need or developed want does this product meet?"

You might use logic if your product is a hard-nosed performer and you can justify the reasons why it is so good. Perhaps it saves both time and money. Fine. You can say that. But don't stop there. Go beyond cold logic into the warmer currents of emotional persuasion. Time saved can become extra time for your consumer to do other things, and extra money can be used for further fulfillments.

Some basic appeals have been mentioned earlier in this book, but you have dozens at your fingertips. The most widely used psychological appeals are:

Sensory: touch, taste, smell, hear, look.

Appetite: conjure up the sizzle along with the steak.

Security: personal or property.

Acquisitiveness: news of money-saving is welcome.

Well-being: good health is a continuous wish; be sure your promises of health benefits are true.

Attractiveness: a universally pursued want.

Threat: implied fear of loss of a benefit currently enjoyed (use with care!)

Humor: lightheartedness attracts and pleases.

Convenience: be sure your product is a genuine help.

Curiosity: an instinctive appeal, be informative.

Ego: self-respect and pride are powerful motivators; a catch-all with many subdivisions.

Nothing is automatic in advertising, not even appeals. Whether explicit or implied, appeals must be honestly based. Over-promise of reward (to ego, security, etc.) might convince someone to buy and try, but disappointment in product performance means no repeat business.

10. If it's news, make it sound important.

Make sure that it *is* news. Too many commercials promising "news" have made listeners wary. If you're to write commercials for the semi-annual white sale at the Bon-Ton, don't regard it as an earthshaking event. Don't make it sound as important as landing on Mars. Keep your news relative to its importance to your prospective customer.

11. Multiply your TV impressions.

If the audio track for your TV spot can double, that is, serve as a radio commercial too, it stretches the ad dollar nicely. When a listener hears a spot he or she has seen on television, it can be instantly visualized (at less cost to the client). "Charlie-the-Tuna" is so familiar on television that a radio spot with sound effects and music and Charlie's familiar voice can give a mental impression of Charlie trying to be chosen for his "good taste." Chevrolet's "Baseball, hot dogs, apple pie and Chevrolet" works in radio and television. It does many things and does them well: establishes the name (count the repetitions), establishes a context, a position (acceptability, friendliness, enjoyment), it entertains, has an infectious rhythm, and delivers information in a pleasant, upbeat manner.

12. Keep a friendly feeling going.

Engage your audience—don't make the listener mad or irritated. Remember, you're trying to win friends as well as influence prospective customers (and reinforce attitudes of current ones). How many grumpy salespeople do you know to be outstanding? This applies not only for your lead-in but also for the entire commercial. Make it smile!

13. Humorous spots had better be funny.

Why does almost every copywriter begin by thinking that the way to sell is to be very, very funny?

Humor just seems easy, but in truth, humor-that-sells is rare. Not every product is amenable to humorous treatment, nor does everyone who listens to radio have a similar sense of humor. Spots with humor may be fun to write, but they are sometimes difficult to get through the client's approval process, and seldom really sell (though they might entertain).

Study the Blue Nun Wine commercial with Stiller and Meara in Chapter 7. It's not only an award winner, delivered in an all-but-extemporized style, but it also sold the product. Top-drawer talent, perfect tone, clear appeal.

14. Give the listener something to do.

The bid for action, usually near the close of a spot, is like a salesman asking for the order. What do you want the listener to do? Where? When? If it's a local spot use an address and ask the listeners to stop in. Immediate action demands a phone number (and repeat it) with some urgency. If it's national, close with your strong selling theme. This gives the listener a final opportunity to react to, and commit to memory, your main appeal.

Chapter 7

Creative Radio Assignments

Advertiser: True Value Hardware Stores   Structure: Straight announcement
Product or service: Sunbeam Hotshot   Commercial length: 60 seconds

Dialogue and directions

Announcer: True Value Hardware Stores suggest you give a Christmas gift that **really** makes instant coffee, soup, or cocoa. Give the Sunbeam Hotshot.

Hi, I'm *(announcer's name)* to tell you that you're really not making instant coffee, soup, or cocoa if you take the time to boil water in a pot. When you use the Sunbeam Hotshot, you get about 12 ounces of hot water in only about 90 seconds with the touch of a lever. That's **really** instant coffee! Plus, it's really convenient when you only want to make one or two cups of the hot beverage.

You'll find the Sunbeam Hotshot at participating True Value Hardware Stores. And you'll recognize it by its compact size, with a cord that stores in the back, and by its attractive Harvest Gold exterior with a rich wood-tone finish front.

So, if you want to give a Christmas gift that **really** makes instant hot beverages, get the Sunbeam Hotshot. Because you're not really making instant coffee if you take the time to boil water in a pot. You'll find it at participating True Value Hardware Stores. Tell 'em *(announcer's name)* sent you.

Analysis of straight announcement commercial for True Value Hardware Stores

Here's a strong example that shows the oldest radio spot format can still be among the most effective. It is easy to listen to. It is hard-hitting. It tells the product name, what it does, and gives a personal reason to buy all in the first 22 words. No music, no sound effects, but plenty of well-crafted identification copy for store and appliance, some quick demonstration copy, and good use of repetition. The "you" is prominent and used in context with some activity. True Value Hardware Stores adds to the listenability of its spots by using a well-known broadcast personality.

RADIO SCRIPT SHEET

Student name: Advertiser:

Date submitted: Product or service:

Commercial length: Structure:

Dialogue and directions

Advertiser: Garvey's Transmissions

Product or service: Transmission service

Structure: Announcer plus sound effects

Commercial length: 60 seconds

Dialogue and directions

Announcer: This is a man in a big hurry.

SFX: Whoosh of jet.

Announcer: He's headed for Garvey's Transmission, at Pike and 28th.

SFX: Horse galloping.

Announcer: He arrives at Garvey's Transmission.

SFX: Screeching brakes.

Announcer: He goes into Garvey's Transmission.

SFX: Wood and glass breaking.

Announcer: He talks to the manager at Garvey's Transmission.

SFX: Speeded-up voices.

Announcer: Now, he doesn't have to worry about laying out a lot of cash or even a down-payment at Garvey's Transmission for any motor or transmission work.

SFX: Cash register.

Announcer: He gets instant credit and easy budget terms with no money down, just like . . .

SFX: Fingers snap.

Announcer: . . . that! When he brought in his car his transmission . . .

SFX: A grinding "clunker."

Announcer: . . . sounded like a cement mixer in reverse. And in only a couple of days . . .

SFX: Ticking of clock.

Announcer: . . . his car will . . .

SFX: Purring cat.

Announcer: He became a happy man . . .

SFX: Laughter.

Announcer: . . . at Garvey's Transmission. And you will, too!

Analysis of Garvey's Transmission commercial

This commercial, without sound effects, would be dull and boring. With exaggerated sound effect interruptions to underline and emphasize both continuity and service points, this spot works at keeping ear interest high. At the same time, it allows frequent mention of the advertiser's name and business, and together the voice and sound effects act to aid recall.

RADIO SCRIPT SHEET

Student Name: Advertiser:

Date submitted: Product or service:

Commercial length: Structure:

Dialogue and directions

Advertiser: French Creek Sheep & Wool Company

Product or service: Sheepskin coats

Structure: Straight announcement with sound effects

Commercial length: 60 seconds

Dialogue and directions

SFX: General outdoor ranch sounds: rustle of leaves, twittering of birds, bleating of sheep, bark of sheepdog. Establish 4 seconds, then down and under voice throughout.

Eric Flaxenburg: One of the most beautiful sights that spring has to offer is a flock of sheep pasturing on a rolling green hillside. I'm Eric Flaxenburg, and I ought to know. Along with my wife, Jean, I own and operate a small Chester County Sheep Ranch . . . the French Creek Sheep & Wool Company . . . where some of the very finest sheepskin coats in the world are made. Handcrafted in the French Creek tradition by people who really love their work. Evidently, most of our regular listeners agree, because the response to our annual sale of sheepskin coats has been nothing short of phenomenal. But we're still hearing from friends who haven't been able to get out to see us yet, so Jean and I have decided to extend the sale just a little longer. To give them . . . and you . . . the chance to save 20 percent on handsome sheepskin coats and jackets for men and women. We'll even custom make you a coat at 10 percent savings if you can't find your coat in stock. Since the price of pelts will probably rise again this fall, this is the perfect chance for you to save substantially on the sheepskin coat you've always wanted to own . . . at French Creek Sheep & Wool Company. For directions and additional information, call 1-286-5700. That's 1-286-5700.

Analysis of commercial for French Creek Sheep & Wool Company

Here is information plus persuasion. The mood and stage are set with the sound effects. They "take" the listener into the country in the first few seconds. The company co-owner, Eric Flaxenburg, speaks in a friendly, well-modulated but conversational tone—as if he were talking with someone he knew quite well. The dialogue is not rushed, each point seems to follow easily from the preceding point. There is an urgency in the possible price rise, and good help in the closing bid for action.

RADIO SCRIPT SHEET

Student name: Advertiser:

Date submitted: Product or service:

Commercial length: Structure:

Dialogue and directions

Advertiser: Schieffelin & Co.   Structure: Slice of life, with humor
Product or service: Blue Nun Wine   Commercial length: 60 seconds

Dialogue and directions

Stiller: Excuse me, the cruise director assigned me this table for dinner.

Meara: Say, weren't you the fella at the costume ball last night dressed as a giant tuna? With scales, the gills and the fins?

Stiller: Yeah—that was me.

Meara: I recognized you right away.

Stiller: Were you there?

Meara: I was dressed as a mermaid so I had to spend most of the night sitting down. Did you ever try dancing with both legs wrapped in aluminum foil?

Stiller: No, I can't say I have. Did you order dinner yet?

Meara: I'm having the filet of sole.

Stiller: Hmmm. The filet mignon looks good. Would you like to share a bottle of wine?

Meara: Terrific.

Stiller: I noticed a little Blue Nun at the Captain's table.

Meara: Poor thing. Maybe she's seasick.

Stiller: No, Blue Nun is a wine. A delicious white wine.

Meara: Oh, we can't have a white wine if you're having meat and I'm having fish.

Stiller: Sure we can. Blue Nun is a white wine that's correct with any dish. Your filet of sole. My filet mignon.

Meara: Oh, it's so nice to meet a man who knows the finer things. You must be a gourmet?

Stiller: No, as a matter of fact, I'm an accountant. Small firm in the city. Do a lot of tax work. . . . *(fade out)*

Announcer: Blue Nun. The delicious white wine that's correct with any dish. Another Sichel wine imported by Schieffelin & Company, New York.

Analysis of commercial for Blue Nun Wine

This slice-of-life example uses the unique humor of established actors in a recognizable situation to introduce the product. It follows the advertising strategy (Blue Nun is the one wine that is correct with any dish) and combines a persuasive reminder with entertainment. What gives this spot uniqueness? The comedic talents of Gerry Stiller and Anne Meara who underplay, speak in natural, conversational tones, and with perfect timing. The main idea comes through clearly, and the commercial is a delight to listen to again and again.

RADIO SCRIPT SHEET

Student Name: Advertiser:

Date submitted: Product or service:

Commercial length: Structure:

Dialogue and directions

Advertiser: Magee's

Product or service: Jeans

Structure: Dialogue plus jingle tag

Commercial length: 60 seconds

Dialogue and directions

Music: Establish light rock rhythm, keep under dialogue.

Man: Hey, Magee's Stone Woman, you still making history?

Woman: I sure hope not.

Man: Listen, Stone Lady, we're worried about your super-cool costume. The winters here are very whippy and we think your little dinosaur dress is going to give you leg cramps. How about if we turn your teeny dress into a **top** and put it over some new jeans from Magee's Junior Girls?

Woman: You trying to change my style?

Man: Now don't be paranoid.

Woman: Para . . . what?

Man: Paranoid. Means clever as a chicken. Many of Magee's new jeans have a gold underwear stitch around the powderhorn pockets and down the side . . .

Woman: Talk **rock!**

Man: Can't. I don't know how. Some have buttons, some front zip, some high-rise, some wide waistbands, some wide legs . . .

Woman: Talk **ROCK!**

Man: I **can't**, Stone Woman, I don't understand your crazy rock talk. Now, many of Magee's junior-girl jeans are by Prophet and Friends . . .

Woman: . . . rock **MUSIC!**

Man: Nah, the Prophet and Friends group makes **jeans**, not music . . . course, you could wear 'em to rock around the campfire on cold nights . . .

Woman: Aha, **that's** rock talk. Your cave or mine?

Jingle: Hey when you wanna be what you wanna be,
why don't you come and see Magee's.
See Magee's, Lincoln and Omaha,
See Magee's.

Music: End.

Analysis of commercial for Magee's

Notice how this commercial reaches for its special audience—junior girls—with an imaginative Rock Stone Age character. One of a continuing series, this spot gets to the product easily and quickly, then uses the time-honored technique of dialogue in which one character doesn't seem to understand what the other (who usually gives the sales pitch) is talking about. This technique keeps the subject alive and developing and the copy points coming until the final fillip. The jingle serves as a strong reminder as well as a bid for action.

RADIO SCRIPT SHEET

Student name: Advertiser:

Date submitted: Product or service:

Commercial length: Structure:

Dialogue and directions

Advertiser: Pan Am

Product or service: Airline service

Structure: Jingle, vocal group, announcer
plus live announcer tag over music

Commercial length: 60 seconds

Dialogue and directions

Music: Small ensemble, upbeat tempo.

Vocal group: Open up your eyes! Hey, look around you.
There's a lot of world you've never seen.

Music: Continue under.

Announcer: There's one airline that can help you change all that. Pan Am. America's airline to the world. To sixty-one countries on all six continents. Anytime you feel you've been waiting around . . . long enough.

Vocal group: Welcome to our world.
Welcome to our world.
Welcome to the world of Pan Am.
America's airline to the world.

Announcer: (Live, local, over music) Going to London or Amsterdam? Pan Am can take you there from Philadelphia three times a week. Just take Airflight to Pan Am's Worldport where you can make connections to Pan Am's 747 to London or Amsterdam. Call your travel agent for reservations.

Analysis of commercial for Pan Am

The tune is pleasant and easy to hum or sing along with. There is a call to the listener to "open up" and "look around" which leads to thoughts of all the places one hasn't seen. The announcer continues the friendly tone with an offer to help with information about Pan Am's far-flung service. As the music builds, the lyrics draw the prospect farther into the Pan Am world. The live tag, delivered over music, gives an advertiser great flexibility. This copy can be changed as often as needed. Nothing unusual in technique, but nevertheless this commercial welds carefully thought-out components into an appealing, seductive message.

RADIO SCRIPT SHEET

Student Name: Advertiser:

Date submitted: Product or service:

Commercial length: Structure:

Dialogue and directions

Advertiser: Australian Trade Commission   Structure: Fact sheet
Product or service: Apples and pears   Commercial length: 30 or 60 seconds

Fact Sheet

Products: Australian apples and pears

1. A fresh supply of Australian apples and pears has just arrived.
2. Two varieties of pears are Bosc and Parkhams (Park-ums).
3. Both are sweet, succulent, with a distinctive taste.
4. They may look like domestic pears, but their taste is superior—their flesh white, aromatic.
5. Pears shipped to the U.S. are the best of a vintage crop.
6. The apples are called "Granny Smith" apples.
7. Green in color, but nevertheless magnificent eating apples.
8. These apples can also be used in cooking.
9. Now available in grocery stores and supermarkets at a price about the same as domestic apples and pears.
10. More and more people are asking for them, so hurry—before they are sold out.

Analysis of fact sheet

Many clients take advantage of the skills of local deejays and/or announcers who are particularly adept at ad-libbing. Rather than restrict them to following a script, they are given fact sheets about the product or service. It is then up to each announcer to provide a lead-in, to lace the different sales points together with attractive continuity, and to provide persuasive word pictures, ending with a strong bid for action. The fact sheet illustrated here supplies the names, descriptions, and uses for the products to be described effectively in an extemporaneous spot.

RADIO SCRIPT SHEET

Student Name: Advertiser:

Date submitted: Product or service:

Commercial length: Structure:

Dialogue and directions

Account A sponsor who has entered into a contract with a station or network; also a contract between a sponsor and an advertising agency or representative.

Across the board Program presented five days a week at the same time each day.

Ad-lib To announce or talk without a prepared script.

AFTRA American Federation of Television and Radio Artists. A national labor organization representing people in radio and television, especially performers (talent).

Aircheck Recording of a program or commercial.

Airman Also called announcer or personality. Someone who is performing on the air (e.g., a disc jockey).

Airshift Or "show" time when talent is on the air.

Allocation The specific assignment of frequency and power to a station by the Federal Communications Commission.

Audition The testing, usually in a studio, of talent for a particular role in a commercial or a specific job for a performance.

Back-timing Timing the last two or three stories of a newscast, speech, or music, etc., in a program to enable the talent to get off the air on time.

Block programming The scheduling of programs of similar appeal back-to-back to keep listeners from switching to another station.

Board The control panel through which the broadcast program passes.

Bulletin The first brief announcement of an important news event.

Call letters Letters assigned to a station by the FCC.

Cart A cassette-type cartridge. Used for taped announcements, jingles, commercials, music, or bridges, etc.

Call letters Letters assigned to a station by the FCC.

Clearing music Obtaining releases (approval) from the copyright holders of music, or ascertaining whether the station, as a result of contracts with organizations holding copyrights (ASCAP, BMI) is privileged to present a musical selection.

Close Closing announcement to a program.

Cluster buster A line or phrase to break up back-to-back commercial announcements.

Commentary A section of a program devoted to opinion.

Commercial Advertising; sometimes called a "spot."

Continuity writer One who creates radio copy other than news.

Cough button Small switch attached to mike or on studio control panel which, when pressed, cuts mike off while talent clears his throat.

Cue A signal, either verbal or by sign. Also, "cue a record," the act of preparing a record to be played on the air without an opening "wow."

Cut a record To make a recording or transcription; also, "make a tape," or "lay down a tape."

Dateline program News program written in bulletin style with each story beginning with the name of the city or location where the story originated.

Dead air Unintentional silence on the air.

DGA Directors Guild of America. A national organization representing film, television, and radio directors.

Drive time Those morning and late-afternoon hours when commuters are driving to and from work.

Dub or dubbing Transferring material from one record or tape to another.

Fade Decrease in volume.

Fading in Increasing volume so that music, sound, or speech rises in volume gradually.

Feedback Return of sound from a loudspeaker to the mike in which it originated; also, public response to station management either in complaint or praise.

Feeding Delivery of a program over a telephone hookup either to a network or some other point.

Fluff A mistake in delivery by talent.

Format Type of programming a station uses (e.g., classical, all news, top forty, MOR, beautiful music).

Frequency discount Discount given by a network or station to a sponsor who buys commercial time in large quantities.

Fuzzy Applies to program or line which is not clear.

Gain Control of volume; usually called "riding gain."

Guideline One-word description of a news story. Also called "slug" or "slugline."

I.D. Station call letters followed by location (e.g., WBCB . . . Levittown-Fairless Hills).

Independent station Local, commercial station not affiliated with any network, usually found in the larger markets.

Jingle Musical commercial for product, service, or station.

Jumping cue When an announcer or newscaster starts a program before he is scheduled to begin.

Level Volume noted upon the meter (potentiometer) of the control board. Knob sometimes called a "pot."

Line Telephone line (wire) used for the transmission of a program.

Live announcement Message read in person, not pre-recorded.

Live mike A microphone that is turned on.

Log A record or schedule of everything broadcast; required by the FCC.

Monitoring Listening to a program.

MOR Format used by many stations featuring middle-of-the-road-type music.

NAB National Association of Broadcasters; a trade organization devoted to promoting radio and TV stations.

NABET National Association of Broadcast Engineers and Technicians; a labor organization.

Nemo A program originating outside of the local studio.

News analyst One who reports, analyzes, and comments on news.

Newscaster One who reads straight news on the air, and who may or may not write his own news for on-air delivery.

News editor One who re-writes, edits, and supervises the news program. May also deliver news on the air.

O & O stations Broadcasting stations "owned and operated" by a network. Usually very successful stations in large markets that contribute handsomely to a network's total profit.

Open Introductory announcement to a program.

Optional copy Additional news items which announcer or newscaster can use if he runs short of copy.

Over modulating Putting too much volume over the air; sometimes called "blasting."

Participating sponsor A client who shares commercial time with other sponsors of the same program.

PBS Public Broadcasting System. Non-profit radio and TV network.

Printer Teletype machine.

Protection An extra take, to be used in case the selected take is ruined or lost.

PSA Public service announcement.

Public domain [or PD] Program or commercial content not protected by copyright that may be used freely without payment of a fee. PD can also mean program director.

RAB Radio Advertising Bureau.

Ratings Statistical measurements of a station's audience.

Reading cold Reading a program or a news story on the air without having rehearsed it.

Release Copy sent in advance to be held for use at a designated time.

Remote A program picked up from outside the studio (e.g., football games, reports from the scene of a fire or flood).

Rewrite A news story or program that undergoes revision.

RTNDA Radio-Television News Directors Association.

Special event On-the-scene broadcast of a news event, usually planned.

Spot A commercial, either recorded or delivered live.

Standby A program used in emergencies.

Stand by A cue to performers before they are given a live microphone.

Station break Or just "break." A pause to permit local stations to identify themselves.

Sustainer A program that is not sponsored.

Tack-up A news program prepared by pasting or stapling wire copy to sheets of copy paper and then editing the stories.

Take A performance attempt. When recording, each attempt is given a number, "Take One," "Take Two," etc. The take deemed most satisfactory is then used.

Talk-over When an airman talks during the first few bars of a musical selection.

Ticket A license granted by the FCC.

Time copy Copy for news or a live commercial that is back-timed.

Traffic A station or network department that receives orders for commercials, makes certain that these get on the air, and then follows up in billing advertisers.

Triple-spotting Running three separate commercials in one commercial time period. The NAB Code prohibits this practice during prime time (evening hours), but many stations triple-spot in the daytime and during fringe evening hours.

Wire copy News, sports, weather and information printed by a teletype machine, usually originating from the Associated Press, United Press International, or another news service.

Woof Sound made by an engineer into a microphone to synchronize audio levels.

WX Symbol for weather.

Section III
Television Commercials

Chapter 9

Importance of Structure

The television viewer's mind is a complex piece of machinery which is capable of being attracted by, paying attention to, and absorbing sales ideas, but only if those ideas are stimulating, relevant, and presented in an interesting and orderly pattern. It is easier to remember ideas that fit into a cohesive form or structure than it is to recall ideas that are unrelated, jumbled together, or overwhelmed by a confusing technique.

The TV viewer is not breathlessly waiting to see your commercial. He couldn't care less. The commercial must not only attract and hold his attention, but it also must arouse his emotional interest and involve him to the point of conviction. The viewer's mind usually seeks the easiest path—often to the refrigerator for refreshment during a dull or confusing commercial. You will lose your sales opportunity if your commercial idea is weak. You will also lose your viewer if the vehicle or structure is nebulous and undefined.

The need for logical development

It follows that a TV commercial which presents its message in a logical sequence of related facts, impressions, and scenes has a better chance of making a viewer react favorably. If a commercial tries to use or explain too many ideas, if words and pictures emerge haphazardly, it is likely to join the 85 percent of advertising which William Bernbach says goes unnoticed.

The research analysis of Gallup & Robinson, a prominent research organization, has long urged simplicity of message in a clear-cut form. Their studies of commercial effectiveness indicate that viewer recall is lessened when multiple ideas are crammed into a TV message. Keep your commercial singular. And give it a sound structure.

In a continuing research study for an important TV advertiser, this fact stood out: commercials with strong, well-defined structures registered much more effectively than those in which there was little or no design. Not only were the better-structured commercials better remembered, there was evidence that they were also superior in influencing the decision to buy.

A structure becomes the backbone, the continuity of your sales message. Rather than act as a restriction, a unified structure, presented with imagination, actually aids the viewer and helps him follow and remember your message.

The main idea

Just as common sense dictates that you should never try to lift too heavy a weight with your back, so too must you be careful never to overload a structure with too many selling facts or impose a variety of techniques.

It is perhaps obvious that a 10-second station break announcement (or I.D.) should contain only one selling idea. With but 8 seconds of audio at your disposal, you have only enough time for a basic claim or selling idea and the product name. Some ingenious advertisers use the same structure, shortened of course, for their I.D.s as they use for their longer commercials.

As you create 20-second, 30-second, minute, and two-minute spots, you will obviously be able to include more entertainment value or further explanation. But even in the longer spots the selling idea is still the prime mover of your prospective customer. A good test of a selling idea, in fact, is to make it work effectively in a short spot.

Careful study of the commercial examples in the next chapter, "Types of Structure," will indicate how and where some of today's top creators of commercials implant the main idea, support it, and in some cases, restate it. From opening fade-in to closing fade-out, the development of the basic selling proposition moves progressively within a tautly conceived structure.

Combinations of structures

Where we use the term "structure," others may

use the labels "form," "format," or even "technique." The word "structure," however, seems more definitive and helpful. All structures should have form; and "technique" more aptly refers to qualities you will use in your commercials including humor, mood, atmosphere, contrast, actors' styles of delivery, animation, and camera and editing effects.

As you view more and more commercials and begin to analyze them, you will note that some spots utilize more than one structure. For example, a basic problem-solution structure ad can be written in a fantasy style or even with satire. Most of the structures are not mutually exclusive. A story line structure ad featuring the use of personality technique can be combined effectively. One, however, dominates; the secondary one can be considered as a technique on close scrutiny.

Many commercials today feature actors as husbands, housewives, or businessmen in the problem-solution structure, and the brand name or company identification used to close the ad may use animation or special effects.

Stated another way, your basic structure is like a foundation for a house; you can build several styles or types of homes above identical foundations.

Which structure to use?

Your decision will depend on a variety of considerations: the product or service, the market, the audience, the production budget, the intended number of exposures of the commercial, etc. Some structures are better-suited to certain kinds of products and are wholly wrong for others. You wouldn't necessarily structure a perfume commercial as you would a lawn-mower spot.

To sum up

Make it easy for your prospective viewer. Use a structure and develop the ad logically. Don't break its back by trying to have it carry too many ideas. Remember that the structure alone will neither compel nor sell; how you develop the commercial and what you add to it can, if it has within it a singular selling idea.

When you have the opportunity to view a film producer's sample reel of commercials, or when you next spend a few hours watching television, notice and evaluate each commercial's structure. Note how many have well-defined structures and how many do not. The best-remembered, the most effective spots will usually be those which have strong, clear-cut structures.

Chapter 10
Types of Structure

STORY LINE

The story-line structure lets you develop a simple "plot" with a beginning, middle, and close. It should be simple, clear, and step-by-step, either in chronological order or flashback.

Each step in the story must relate to and follow the point that has gone before. Keep the story line simple. Build interest by keeping the outcome a pleasant surprise. But when you build to a climax or resolution, take care not to overbuild. An anti-climax is a let-down; it destroys conviction.

Psychologists recognize that, as a principle of learning, a "rewarded" performance is more likely to be remembered than an unrewarded performance. So make sure your story relates to a viewer's problem (personal appearance, cleaner home, etc.) and offers a viewer reward. Give it good pace; don't let the story lag or the viewer's interest will, too.

Guidelines for developing commercials using the story-line structure:

1. Keep your plot simple and easy to follow.
2. Base it on a truth or a believable situation that can be quickly identified.
3. Create an opening sequence that piques the viewer's curiosity.
4. When you introduce the product or solution, be sure you have prepared the viewer with a situation that requires your solution.
5. Do not rush into a list of product benefits. Choose benefits that relate to the unresolved situation.
6. This structure must have a beginning, a middle developmental section, and an end or resolution. Remember, you are telling a story.
7. Be sure to register your product's name.

Structure: **STORY LINE**

Prudential—"Calamity Chain"

Marketing strategy:

To create an awareness among adults that a Prudential agent can provide not only life insurance coverage but also automobile and homeowner insurance through Prudential's property and casualty divisions.

Advertising objective:

To announce the fact that Prudential is now in the property and casualty business as well as in life insurance. And to state that Prudential may be able to save the consumer money on car and home insurance.

Credits

Advertising Agency: Ted Bates, New York

(MUSIC UNDER) (SFX UNDER) MAN: Hi! Honey. What's new?

WOMAN: Well, the fire's out.

MAN: Fire? WOMAN: We'll have to re-do the kitchen.

WOMAN: But they're coming for the car. MAN: Car? What car? WOMAN: Our car.

MAN: Honey...WOMAN: But at least the plumber's ankle is okay. MAN: The plumber's ankle?

WOMAN: Yeah. He was fixing the faucet when the fire broke out. MAN: Honey...

MAN: Honey, call...call Prudential. WOMAN: Life Insurance?

ANNCR: (VO) Now a Prudential agent can provide insurance for your car and your home.

Same Prudential planning and service. WOMAN: It's all taken care of.

ANNCR: (VO) Most claims are settled with a phone call.

And some people even save money by changing to Prudential for Car and Homeowner's Insurance.

WOMAN: It's nice to save money. MAN: With someone you know.

WOMAN: By the way, guess who bit the mailman.

CHORUS: Get a piece of the Rock.

ANNCR: (VO) Prudential Insurance. (MUSIC OUT)

Student Assignment

Student Assignment Number _____

Use the advertising/marketing information and objectives provided for the commercial on the preceding pages. Write a script and sketch the storyboard for a follow-up TV commercial in this campaign. Use the _____ structure.

Student Name:

Advertiser:

Title of Commercial:

Length of Commercial:

Video:

Audio:

Video:

Audio:

Video:

Audio:

PROBLEM-SOLUTION

You begin with a viewer-oriented problem which is seemingly caused by a product failure to perform. The consequences must seem important and involve negative circumstances—worry, fear, economic or social setback, unsatisfaction. Your hero of a product is introduced, demonstrated, or used, and the results are satisfying. Register the satisfaction.

At its most basic: Barbara has a laundry problem. Her neighbor tells her about a product that has worked well for her. Barbara tries the product. It solves her problem and, not so incidentally, wins praise from peers or husband and children.

It differs from the slice-of-life structure in that your actor might talk to the camera (audience), a voice-over announcer might introduce the product, and special effects devices might dramatize the entrance or demonstration of the product. Because it is such a widely-used structure it needs careful crafting to avoid appearing hackneyed. A unique musical signature or sound effect in synchronization with a distinctive visual device may help.

Guidelines for developing commercials using the problem-solution structure:

1. The problem. State it in terms the viewer can understand, believe, and relate to. Give a sense of actuality to the characters and situation. (Even humor or satire must have a basis in actuality.)

2. The means. Demonstrate the qualities of the product as dramatically as possible, and state the claims clearly. Confine your script to claims that relate to the problem.

3. Seek an uncontrived introduction of the product. Make it as natural as possible, quickly following evidence of the protagonist's dilemma, dissatisfaction, and frustration.

4. Product benefits should be presented between the time the product is introduced and the problem is solved. And, of course, the points should be directed to the solution of the problem.

5. Satisfaction for protagonist and viewer is a must. But do more. Your payoff should include a reward, such as the praise of others, without being flamboyantly dramatic.

6. Be sure to register your product's name.

Structure: **PROBLEM-SOLUTION**

Xerox Corporation—"Monks"

Marketing strategy:

To expand the usage of Xerox machines to central reproduction centers characterized by high volume duplicating. To compete in this market, a new high speed machine with automatic collating capability was developed.

Advertising objectives:

To achieve awareness of the new machine. To communicate that Xerox is an advanced technology company, a good corporate citizen, and a company whose advertising is distinctive and memorable.

Credits

Client: Xerox Corporation
Client Supervisor: Walter L. Olesen
Agency: Needham, Harper & Steers Advertising, Inc.
Art Director: Allen Kay
Writer: Steve Penchina
Producer: Syd Rangell
Production House: Lovenger, Tardio & Melsky
Director: Neil Tardio

(Xerox is a registered trademark of Xerox Corporation.)

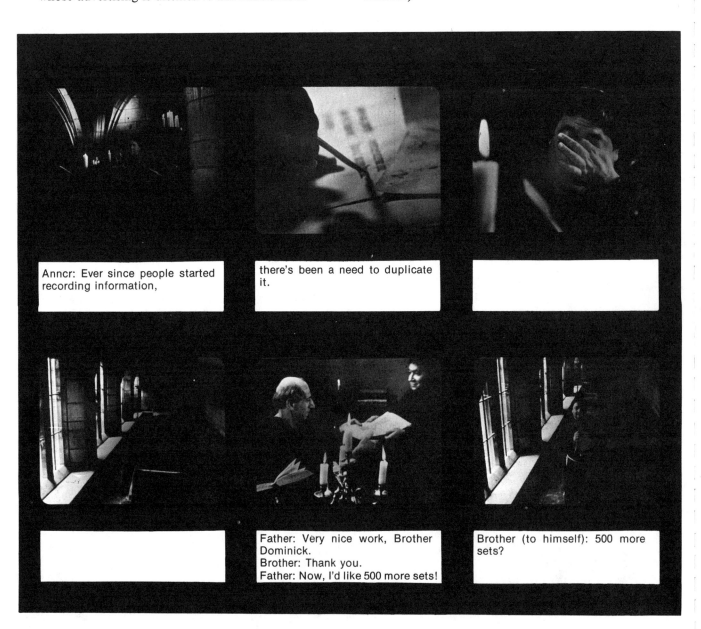

Anncr: Ever since people started recording information,

there's been a need to duplicate it.

Father: Very nice work, Brother Dominick.
Brother: Thank you.
Father: Now, I'd like 500 more sets!

Brother (to himself): 500 more sets?

Stephens: Brother Dominick, what can I do for you?

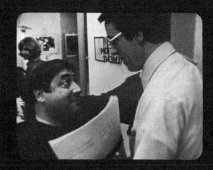

Brother: Could you do a big job for me?

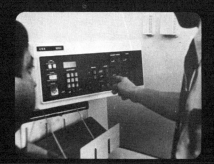

Announcer, V.O.: Xerox has developed an amazing machine that's unlike anything we've ever made. The Xerox 9200 Duplicating

System. It automatically feeds and cycles originals . . . Has a computerized programmer that coordinates the entire system.

Can duplicate, reduce and assemble a virtually limitless number of complete sets . . .

Brother: Here are your sets, Father.
Father: What?
Bro.: The 500 sets you asked for.

Father: It's a miracle!

Student Assignment

Student Assignment Number _____

Use the advertising/marketing information and objectives provided for the commercial on the preceding pages. Write a script and sketch the storyboard for a follow-up TV commercial in this campaign. Use the _____ structure.

Student Name:

Advertiser:

Title of Commercial:

Length of Commercial:

Video:

Audio:

Video:

Audio:

Video:

Audio:

TESTIMONIAL

Someone likes a product, uses it, is satisfied, and tells others about it. When a celebrity tells others, his or her recommendation gains attention for your commercial and interest in your product. If the balance of the spot is pleasant, informative, and promising, the extra fee could be worth it. You should match product and celebrity carefully, and they must have used the product. The viewer must also believe the natural words, attitude, circumstance, and setting.

Effective testimonials can be created with "unknowns," too. An "average" consumer in a store, home, garage, can recommend a detergent, a rug cleaner, an oil filter—whatever—and create a sense of credibility. Most viewers can relate to peer recommendations. A testimonial might be structured in story-line, slice-of-life, or problem-solution form. Or the camera might be hidden to catch true spontaneity. When the actual words of the testifier are used, the nearest approach to word-of-mouth advice, it is more naturally persuasive.

Guidelines for developing commercials using the testimonial structure:

1. Match your product with a believable celebrity, someone who would use the product— and speak well of it.
2. Study and get to know the celebrity's mannerisms and style and pattern of speech. Mold the commercial to suit his delivery.
3. Don't choose a luminary who is being seen to excess in commercials; such overexposure diminishes his credibility with viewers.
4. If the testimonial comes from an expert in his field, and this field relates to your product, your commercial should be much more effective than with a non-expert.
5. Your celebrity should not be bothered with or buried by busy sets, lights, and too many moves.
6. Whether you use a celebrity or an unknown, work for sincerity and believability. Get your commercial to sound like a friend's advice.
7. Be sure to register the name of your product.

Structure: **TESTIMONIAL**
Glidden—"Sarah Wilcox"

Marketing strategy:

Research shows that "prior experience with the brand" and "advice of a friend or relative" are two of the strongest influences on a consumer's preference for any given paint brand. We felt that a candid-camera testimonial campaign would vicariously provide these influences since a real user, almost like a friend or relative, would recount his or her prior experiences with Glidden.

Advertising objective:

Using the hidden-camera technique, three goals were sought:

1. To convincingly present the quality of various product attributes of Glidden paints through testimonials by real consumers.
2. To demonstrate the fierce brand loyalty that exists among Glidden users.
3. To create strong believability for Glidden advertising.

Credits

Advertiser: Glidden-Durkee Division of SCM Corporation
Agency: Meldrum and Fewsmith
Writer: Bruce Stauderman
Producer: Bruce Stauderman
Production House: Panel Films
Director: Henry Knaup

Mrs. Wilcox: My husband kept saying, 'Gee, this is just like a milk shake!'

You know, it just goes on like . . . like a dream.

Interviewer: (V.O.) Here's house-wife, Sarah Wilcox, talking about Glidden Spred Satin:

Mrs. Wilcox: My husband would say, 'Honey, you put two coats

up.' And the first coat he put up and said, 'Well, probably won't

cover all over, so, we'll want to put a second coat on.'

And it dried, and we didn't have to put a second coat on. — Glidden

Spred Satin is, ah, very easy to use. And the results are excellent!

Interviewer: Glidden Spred Satin. A paint you can be loyal to.

Student Assignment

Student Assignment Number _____

Use the advertising/marketing information and objectives provided for the commercial on the preceding pages. Write a script and sketch the storyboard for a follow-up TV commercial in this campaign. Use the _____ structure.

Student Name:

Advertiser:

Title of Commercial:

Length of Commercial:

Video:

Audio:

Video:

Audio:

Video:

Audio:

SPOKESMAN

The use of an on-camera announcer to speak directly to television viewers about a sponsor's product dates from the first days of television. In its simplest form, it is a straight radio announcement illustrated by a moving picture of an announcer and the product. Although it is sometimes enlivened by demonstrations, it is basically "talk," which may be fast, hard-sell, or more personal and intimate.

Direct, "personal" contact between a spokesman and the viewer is a valuable and generally economical device. The message is straightforward and simple; there is little to distract the viewer from the exhortation to learn about the product and to buy it. This structure has the force of the spokesman's personality behind it. Many effective network commercials use this technique with a "name" announcer. In fact, Ed McMahon built a career out of his ability to project a warmth and personal conviction about a product. These are the qualities which give this structure its selling strength.

Guidelines for developing commercials using the spokesman structure:

1. Use great care in casting your announcer/spokesman. Personality is an intangible. The announcer who strikes some viewers as overbearing, funny, or weak may elicit different reactions from others. Your spokesman should be a personal and personable reflection of the product and its manufacturer.

2. Write the copy in easy, conversational style. It must seem to be extemporaneous, sincere, and believable. Avoid long, complex sentences. Don't crowd the copy with too many ideas. People don't pay attention that closely.

3. Try for an out-of-the-ordinary concept or execution. Can the background be made more interesting? Can you include a demonstration? Will extreme close-ups add interest?

4. If you use a well-known personality, write in his or her style. Take advantage of his charm, personality, and persuasiveness.

5. Consider carefully whether a man or a woman would be a more effective person to sell the product.

6. Be sure to register the name of your product.

Structure: **SPOKESMAN**

Alpo—"ALPO Time"

Marketing strategy:

From the beginning, Alpo has been positioned as high quality, all-meat dog food, a "natural" favorite of all types of dogs.

Advertising objective:

To convince dog food users, primarily those using canned dog food, that Alpo is good for dogs for two reasons. First, it has a high level of beef and meat by-products. And second, Alpo is a complete and balanced diet.

Credits

Advertiser: Alpo
Advertising agency: Weightman, Inc.
Writer: Maureen Hall
Producer: Bob Harris
Production House: Mort Kasman Productions

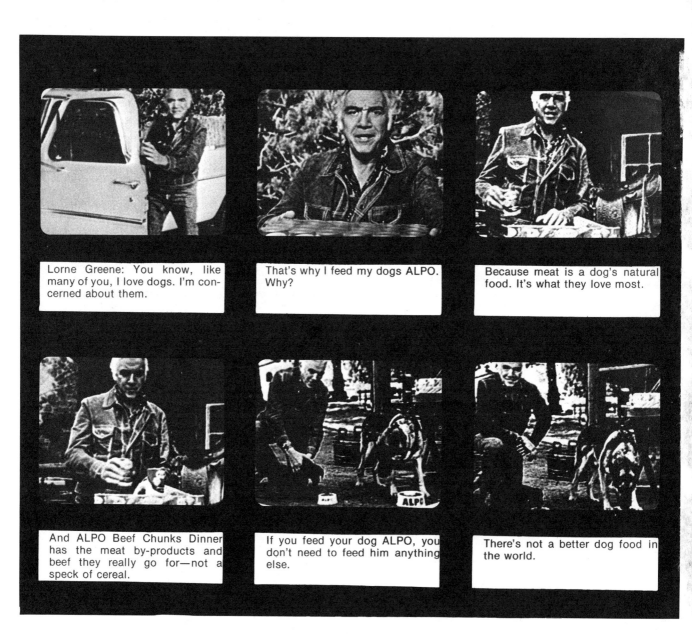

Lorne Greene: You know, like many of you, I love dogs. I'm concerned about them.

That's why I feed my dogs ALPO. Why?

Because meat is a dog's natural food. It's what they love most.

And ALPO Beef Chunks Dinner has the meat by-products and beef they really go for—not a speck of cereal.

If you feed your dog ALPO, you don't need to feed him anything else.

There's not a better dog food in the world.

Lorne Greene: You want to see something? Watch this.

C'mon. ALPO Time! ALPO Time!

Look at 'em. Every natural instinct tells 'em they should eat meat. And you know something? Their instincts are abosolutely *right*.

Meat is good for dogs. Full of protein, energy, nourishment. I feed my dogs ALPO Beef Chunks Dinner because it's meat by-products,

beef and balanced nutrition.

ALPO's all a dog ever needs to eat.

There's no better dog food in the world.

Student Assignment

Student Assignment Number _____

Use the advertising/marketing information and objectives provided for the commercial on the preceding pages. Write a script and sketch the storyboard for a follow-up TV commercial in this campaign. Use the _____ structure.

Student Name:

Advertiser:

Title of Commercial:

Length of Commercial:

Video:

Audio:

Video:

Audio:

Video:

Audio:

DEMONSTRATION

Television provides the unique opportunity to do what no other mass communication medium can do: show actual proof of a product performance claim. TV advertising, from the very beginning, has taken good advantage of this opportunity. An effective demonstration leaves little doubt in a viewer's mind about a product's performance. There's no better way to help overcome sales resistance.

Interesting demonstrations are a TV commercial's best friend. They hold attention, prove a product's superiority, and convince the viewer. And, of course, they score extremely well in terms of viewer involvement. All research agrees on this. Nothing convinces a prospective customer faster and better than actually showing him that a product does what it claims to do. A series of studies for one advertiser proved that a demonstration claim was not only better remembered than a claim made only verbally, but that the entire commercial message was better remembered.

One cautionary word. If you use a demonstration, you must be absolutely certain that it is a true and authentic demonstration.

Guidelines for developing commercials using the demonstration structure:

1. Don't try to fool the viewer. Keep the camera on the demonstration from start to finish if you can. Cutting away, then back again, offers viewers a chance to doubt.

2. Use close-ups and extreme close-ups for demonstrations whenever you can.

3. Make your demonstration meaningful and relevant. Help the viewer by giving him the message simply and directly.

4. Repeat the demonstration many times in dry runs before you begin to create the commercial. Time it again and again so that you know precisely the number of seconds you have to work with. This practice will also show you just how effectively the demonstration comes across on camera.

5. The significance of the demonstration must be made clear to the viewer. Keep the words simple, let the viewer know what is happening, and make the results rewarding.

6. After writing your demonstration spot, ask an associate to read the video portion only. He should be able to understand the main message without referring to the audio.

7. Be sure to register the product's name.

Structure: **DEMONSTRATION**
Elmer's Glue-All—"Bulldozer"

Marketing strategy:

To position Elmer's Glue-All as the best all-purpose household adhesive for repair projects.

Advertising objective:

To convince consumers of the superior strength of Elmer's Glue-All on common household materials by illustrating its strength through the use of a dramatic demonstration.

Credits

Advertising agency: Conahay & Lyon, Inc.

Look. The Elmer's held.

Elmer's was stronger than the wood itself.

Stronger than you'll ever need for most household jobs.

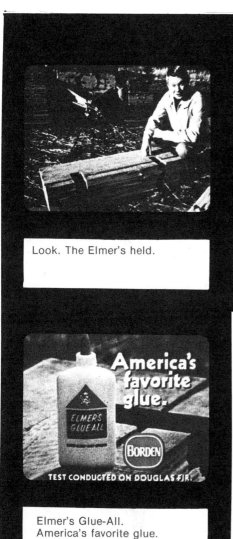

Elmer's Glue-All.
America's favorite glue.

Student Assignment

Student Assignment Number _____

Use the advertising/marketing information and objectives provided for the commercial on the preceding pages. Write a script and sketch the storyboard for a follow-up TV commercial in this campaign. Use the _____ structure.

Student Name:

Advertiser:

Title of Commercial:

Length of Commercial:

Video:

Audio:

Video:

Audio:

Video:

Audio:

SUSPENSE

The opening and early portions of a commercial using suspense should attract and intrigue the viewer, but not give away the secret at the heart of the ad. (The product is usually depicted as a "helpful hero.") Both audio and video should build anticipation. Other structures do this, but not to the degree of a truly suspenseful commercial.

The suspense should be related to the product, its performance, and the viewer's benefit. The copy generally prepares the viewer, generates a "what's going to happen?" attitude. At the payoff the strongest sales point should be made—and proved or demonstrated. Not all sales stories lend themselves to this structure. It is difficult to write, needs an eye-catching *and sustaining* visual move or device, and must have a climax worth the viewer's wait.

Guidelines for developing commercials using the suspense structure:

1. Begin the suspense immediately, build it carefully, end it with clarity and relevance so that it rewards the viewer.
2. Make sure that all the important points of the sales message relate to the suspense and that your key point is held for the payoff.
3. Make characters and settings work for the product clearly and simply. Don't cloud or cloak the one strong point you wish to make.
4. Pacing is all-important in suspense. Keep the ad building, working. Allow enough time at the end for an adequate payoff.
5. Consider ending the spot with a suspense-relieving punchline if humor is used. A switch ending should neither detract from a viewer's belief not cause him to feel cheated or duped.
6. At the climax, your product should clearly be the hero, the best answer to a problem; or if your protagonist is the hero, he must fit that role because of the advantages of the product.
7. Be sure to register your product's name.

Structure: **SUSPENSE**

Heinz—"Ketchup Race"

Marketing strategy:

To position Heinz Ketchup to consumers as thicker and richer (therefore, more flavorful) than other brands.

Advertising objective:

To demonstrate, as convincingly as possible, the thickness and richness of Heinz against a leading competitor.

Credits

Advertiser: Heinz
Advertising agency: Doyle Dane Bernbach, Inc.
Writer: Francine Wexler
Art director: Bert Steinhauser

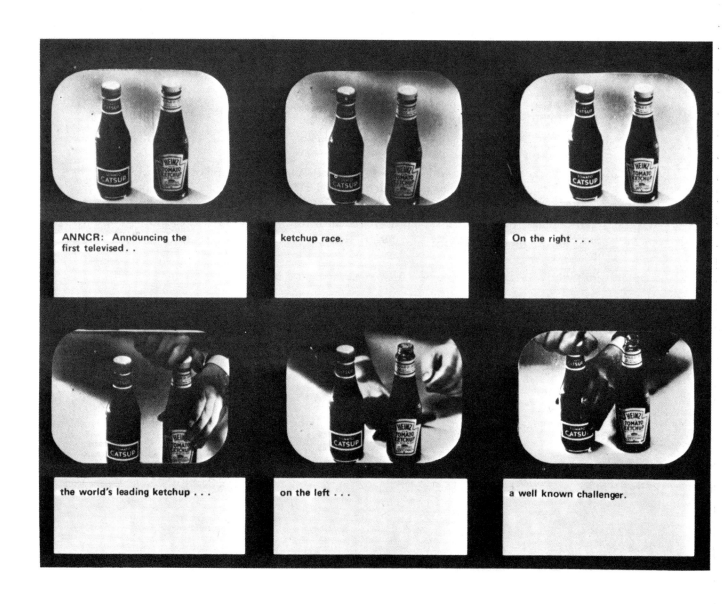

ANNCR: Announcing the first televised . .

ketchup race.

On the right . . .

the world's leading ketchup . . .

on the left . . .

a well known challenger.

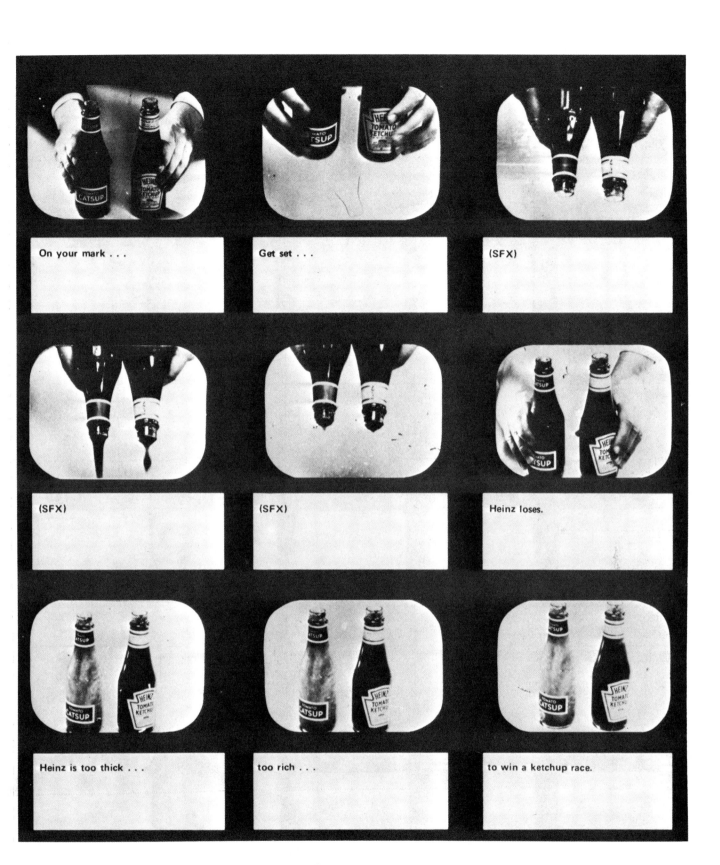

On your mark . . .

Get set . . .

(SFX)

(SFX)

(SFX)

Heinz loses.

Heinz is too thick . . .

too rich . . .

to win a ketchup race.

Student Assignment

Student Assignment Number _____

Use the advertising/marketing information and objectives provided for the commercial on the preceding pages. Write a script and sketch the storyboard for a follow-up TV commercial in this campaign. Use the _____ structure.

Student Name:

Advertiser:

Title of Commercial:

Length of Commercial:

Video:

Audio:

Video:

Audio:

Video:

Audio:

SLICE OF LIFE

The name of this structure is all but self-explanatory. A slice-of-life commercial begins with a person at the point of, and just before the discovery of an answer to, a problem. Emotions run high, and reaction is personal. The trouble may be dandruff, bad breath, less-than-white laundry, or whatever. Most of these commercials center on some personal, household, or business problem. The protagonist may know of his problem or may be told about it. The product is introduced, extolled, and tried. Just before the final urge to buy, we see and are told that the new user is now a better or happier person for it.

The slice-of-life format has been the bread-and-butter structure of top spenders in television since the beginning of TV advertising. Detergent manufacturers use this technique—sometimes perhaps overuse it—but they make it work, and work hard.

Generally, actors are placed in "real" life situations and the problem emerges immediately. The product is introduced by another actor (portraying a friend, relative, coincidental expert, etc.) rather than by a visual device and voice-over announcer as in a problem-solution commercial. Naturalness and believability are goals of the actors' dialogue.

Guidelines for developing commercials using the slice-of-life structure:

1. Involve your viewer at the outset. Make him realize, at once, that the actor's problem is acute and personal. Therefore, it can be an acute and personal problem to the viewer as well.

2. Make your characters as real as possible. Make their situations believable and important. Don't make your protagonist too much of a dolt.

3. Introduce the product in a natural way. Don't force-feed the audience or jolt them into disbelief. The cliche of the neighbor with Brand X at hand in the ever-present shopping bag is just that—a cliche.

4. Good use of humor in writing and judicious casting will allow you to eliminate much of the boredom and bromide from this structure. The whole spot need not be a barrel of laughs, but sly, subtle humor can give this spot memorability and can actually buttress the selling idea.

5. Be sure to register your product's name.

Structure: **SLICE OF LIFE**

Sony—"Multi"

Marketing strategy:

1. To reach a greater number of potential buyers through the medium of prime-time television.
2. To encourage dealers and distributors to carry the full line of Sony products, and to support those that already do.
3. To increase the public's awareness of Sony as a total home electronics manufacturer.

Advertising objectives:

1. To show Sony as a manufacturer of a full range of home electronics products.
2. To support and enhance Sony's quality image through pride of ownership.
3. To continue to present Sony products in a human setting (i.e., slice-of-life action).

Credits

Advertiser: Sony
Advertising agency: Doyle Dane Bernbach, Inc.
Account supervisor: Joe Laun
Writer: Michael Honig
Art director: John Caggiano
Agency producer: Frank DiSalvo
Production House: Rick Levine, N.Y.

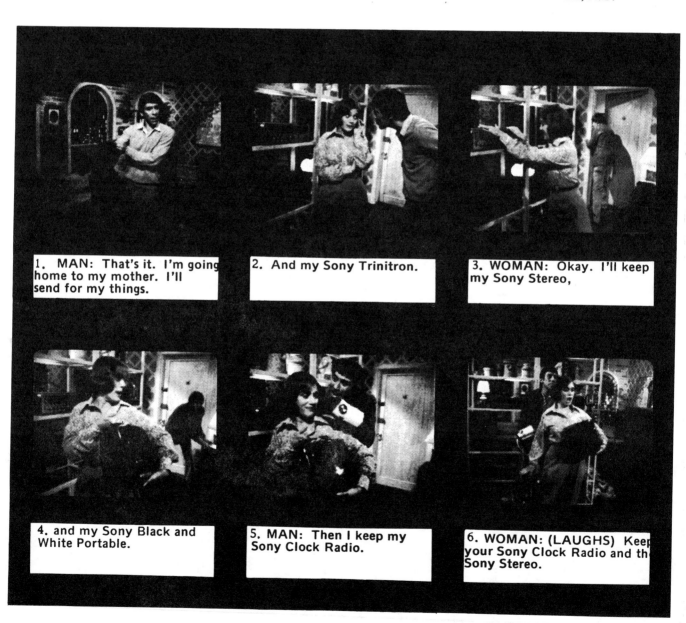

1. MAN: That's it. I'm going home to my mother. I'll send for my things.

2. And my Sony Trinitron.

3. WOMAN: Okay. I'll keep my Sony Stereo,

4. and my Sony Black and White Portable.

5. MAN: Then I keep my Sony Clock Radio.

6. WOMAN: (LAUGHS) Keep your Sony Clock Radio and the Sony Stereo.

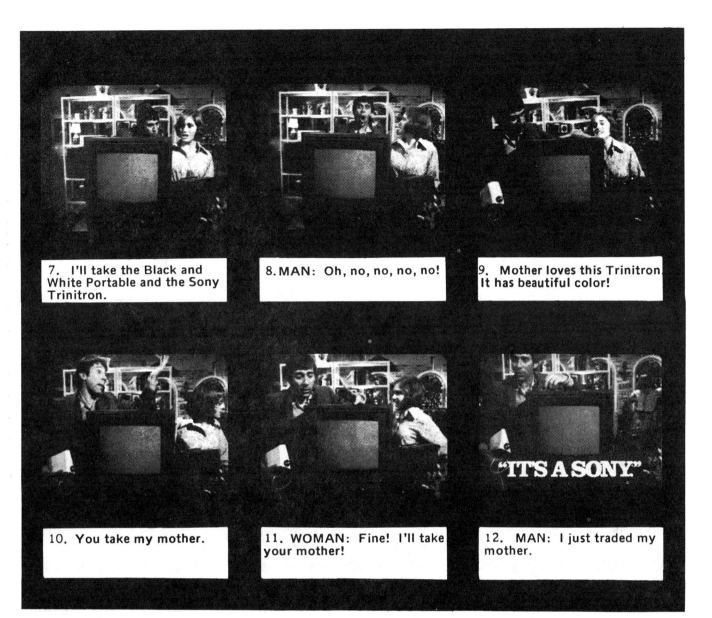

7. I'll take the Black and White Portable and the Sony Trinitron.

8. MAN: Oh, no, no, no, no!

9. Mother loves this Trinitron. It has beautiful color!

10. You take my mother.

11. WOMAN: Fine! I'll take your mother!

12. MAN: I just traded my mother.

Student Assignment

Student Assignment Number _____

Use the advertising/marketing information and objectives provided for the commercial on the preceding pages. Write a script and sketch the storyboard for a follow-up TV commercial in this campaign. Use the _____ structure.

Student Name:

Advertiser:

Title of Commercial:

Length of Commercial:

Video:

Audio:

Video:

Audio:

Video:

Audio:

ANALOGY

An analogy is defined as "a relation of likeness between two things . . . not of the things themselves, but of two or more attributes, circumstances, or effects." In a commercial, you use something with a quality or attribute that relates to your product, and show that relationship. It is indirect comparison, persuasion by implication.

For the viewer to make the inference the analogy must be clear and relevant. A race horse's speed and sleekness have been compared to a car. A rose wine has been advertised: "It's like taking a trip to Portugal." Note that each analogy is pleasant, even romantic. suggestions should be emotionally or logically based, but the reward to the viewer should be pleasant.

Viewers are often unwilling to exert the effort to follow complicated comparisons. An analogy, to work, should be immediately clear and easy to accept. It should give your product a shining image.

Guidelines for developing commercials using the analogy structure:

1. Make certain that the analogous example is one that is familiar and understandable to most viewers.

2. Don't expect the analogy to communicate the message all by itself. Help it with a more direct expression of what you really want to say. Inductive reasoning, in which a viewer is asked to infer a message is a more difficult mental process than deductive reasoning in which the viewer is led through a series of related facts to an inescapable conclusion.

3. Spend little time on your comparative example. Use it merely as a springboard for your product's advantages and benefits. Otherwise, the viewer may recall only your comparative example.

4. Be sure to register your product's name.

Structure: **ANALOGY**

Connecticut General Life Insurance Co.—"Sandcastle"

Marketing strategy:

To reach the high-middle and upper socio-economic prospects for estate planning.

Advertising objective:

1. To illustrate the necessity for sound, solid estate planning including insurance.
2. To present CG's thorough, painstaking, time-taking, and successful method of preparing complicated estate plans.

3. To suggest that the viewer immediately think of his own estate's future and call CG for advice.

Credits

Advertiser: Connecticut General Life Insurance Company
Advertising Agency: Cunningham & Walsh, Inc.
Writer: Normany Cary
Art director: Richard Burton
Producer: Paul Burgraff

(SILENT) (SFX: CRASH OF WAVE)

(SFX: CRASH OF WAVES, CRIES OF SEA GULLS) ANNCR: (VO) A man can work all his life to build up an estate ... and then ...

(SFX: SOUNDS OF SURF, ETC. UP) (SFX: SURF AND SEAGULLS UNDER AND THROUGHOUT)

ANNCR: (VO) How do you make sure your castle is the one that doesn't crumble?

By protecting your estate with the expert help of a Connecticut General man.

He'll work out a solid financial plan for your personal and business needs.

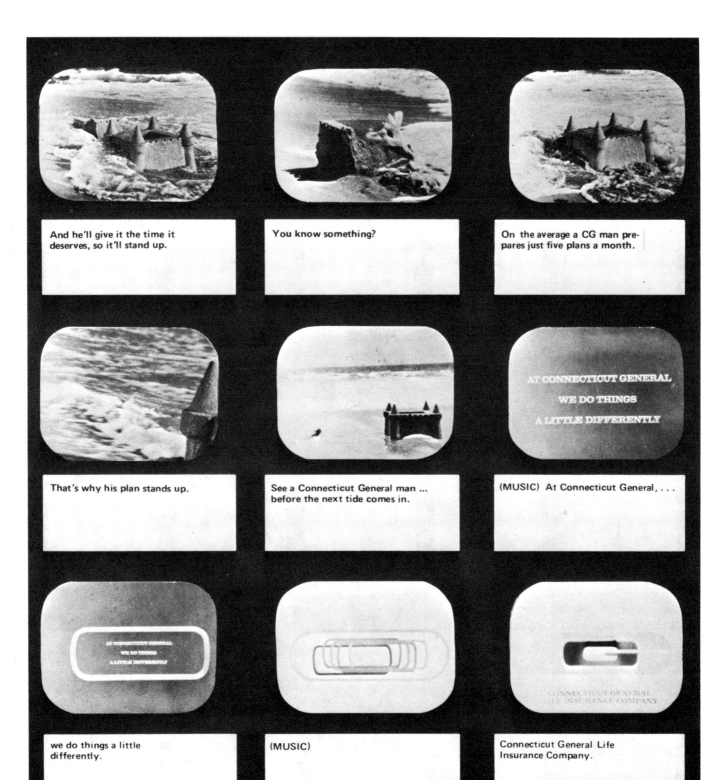

And he'll give it the time it deserves, so it'll stand up.

You know something?

On the average a CG man prepares just five plans a month.

That's why his plan stands up.

See a Connecticut General man ... before the next tide comes in.

(MUSIC) At Connecticut General, ...

we do things a little differently.

(MUSIC)

Connecticut General Life Insurance Company.

Student Assignment

Student Assignment Number _____

Use the advertising/marketing information and objectives provided for the commercial on the preceding pages. Write a script and sketch the storyboard for a follow-up TV commercial in this campaign. Use the _____ structure.

Student Name:

Advertiser:

Title of Commercial:

Length of Commercial:

Video:

Audio:

Video:

Audio:

Video:

Audio:

FANTASY

Successful campaigns have used animated green giants, white knights, and other characters and special effects to create a make-believe world. Here, the product can be made, grown, or consumed—happily. This structure is not entertainment alone. Even though you suspend a viewer's disbelief, the purpose is to fantasize and idealize some attribute of your product.

Audiences have been conditioned to accept fantasy since early childhood, a fact well-noted by cereal manufacturers. A fantasy ad can convey charm and amusement, but never lose sight of the selling proposition or the product.

Techniques vary from animation ("Charlie the Tuna") to exaggerated realism (a cough sufferer destroying his house), from giantism (a super large product and small live announcer showing it) to clowns (Ronald McDonald). Keep on target if you use symbolism. Don't obscure the persuasion with technique. Do use distinctive music and/or sound effects.

Guidelines for developing commercials using fantasy:

1. Make the fantasy treatment relevant to the viewer. Your commercial should mean something, have a reason for being. Entertainment alone is not enough.

2. A musical background makes fantasy more intriguing, more involving. Select music to fit the exact mood of the fantasy.

3. If your commercial tells a story, make the fantasy relate to your product. Do not let it obscure the selling idea. Similarly, the technique or device used should have relevance to the product.

4. Beware of overpowering tricks that may dim your sales message. Tie the technique in with your product for strong registration.

5. Be sure to register your product's name.

Structure: **FANTASY**

Green Giant—"Bean/Nib"

Marketing strategy:

   To help support the national introduction of Kitchen Sliced Green Beans and maintain Niblets Corn consumer franchise.

Advertising objective:

   To position Green Giant Brand canned vegetables (and two products specifically) nationally as a line of superior quality products.

Credits

   Advertiser: Green Giant Co.
Advertising agency: Leo Burnett Co., Inc.
Written and produced by
the staff of Leo Burnett Co.

Green Giant and Green Giant Kitchen Sliced Beans and the Giant figure are trademarks of the Green Giant Company, G.G.Co.®

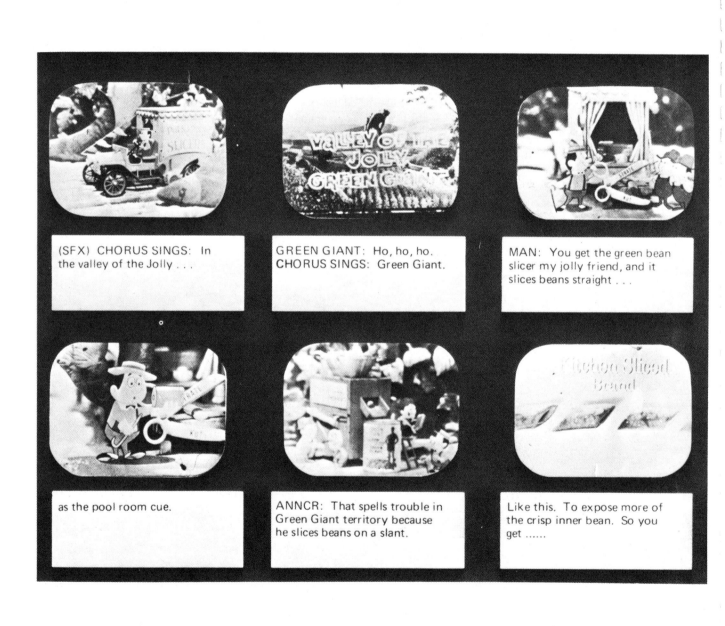

(SFX) CHORUS SINGS: In the valley of the Jolly . . .

GREEN GIANT: Ho, ho, ho.
CHORUS SINGS: Green Giant.

MAN: You get the green bean slicer my jolly friend, and it slices beans straight . . .

as the pool room cue.

ANNCR: That spells trouble in Green Giant territory because he slices beans on a slant.

Like this. To expose more of the crisp inner bean. So you get . . . . . .

CHORUS SINGS: Young beans, snapin' fresh, sliced the way they taste the best.

ANNCR: Try Kitchen Sliced Brand Diagonal Cut Green Beans.

The Green Giant also takes tender kernels of his Niblets corn and puts them up . . .

with almost no water. Then Niblets corn is vacuum packed (SFX) to stay crisp.

Only the Green Giant gives you niblets Brand corn.

CHORUS SINGS: Good things from the garden, . . .

garden, . . .

garden in the valley.

Valley of the Jolly . . .
GREEN GIANT: Ho, Ho, Ho. CHORUS SINGS: Green Giant.

Student Assignment

Student Assignment Number _____

Use the advertising/marketing information and objectives provided for the commercial on the preceding pages. Write a script and sketch the storyboard for a follow-up TV commercial in this campaign. Use the _____ structure.

Student Name:

Advertiser:

Title of Commercial:

Length of Commercial:

Video:

Audio:

Video:

Audio:

Video:

Audio:

PERSONALITY

The personality structure is a technical variant of the spokesman type of commercial (where the announcer is on camera for a straight sell). With the personality structure, an actor plays a character who talks about the product, reacts to its use, or demonstrates its use or enjoyment directly to the camera. This technique relies on an actor or actress who can command attention and interest with a distinctive characterization—a unique voice or delivery, age or appearance.

The actor or actress can be well-known or unknown, but he or she is acting a role, not giving a testimonial *per se*. Attention is gained and interest held almost solely by the actor and his involvement with the product. The success of this technique depends chiefly on the actor's projection of his role, the empathy he arouses in the viewer.

Pleasant humor, the type that wears well, can be a big plus. The humor should definitely not try to overpower. In many commercials of this type, a closing sight gag or punch line gives the spot a delightful fillip—and aids recall and association.

Guidelines for developing commercials using the personality structure:

1. Suit your character to the product, either as protagonist or antagonist, but make it apparent which side he is on.
2. Since this is not a story-line development, you must gain and hold attention through the strengths of your character's personality and involvement with the product. Don't waste time with a build-up. Your opening seconds are all-important.
3. With your character firmly in mind (and on paper) decide whether the commercial would be more effective with a well-known actor or an unknown.
4. If you use humor, do not lay it on heavily. Aim for one great line to use as a payoff.
5. Keep the background relevant but simple, and use closeups.
6. Be sure to register your product's name.

Structure: **PERSONALITY**

Mott's Applesauce—"Schoolboy"

Marketing strategy:

To introduce a new exclusive style of Mott's Applesauce, specifically Golden Delicious Chunky. And in certain markets to use this product as a wedge to gain distribution on all types of sauce.

Advertising strategy:

To leave the consumer with the net impression that regardless of the style or type he or she desires,

Mott's makes that style and makes it better than anyone else.

Credits

Advertiser: Mott's
Advertising agency: Rumrill-Hoyt, Inc.
Writer: Jerome Greenberg
Producer: Lawrence Katz
Art director: Anthony Pugliesi

(SILENT)

CHILD: Apple Sauce by Motts . . .

the best apple sauce in the whole world is made by Motts.

There's Motts Regular . . .

(SILENT)

and Motts Low Calorie . . .

(SILENT)

and Cinnamon . . .

Cinnamon Flavored . . .

Country Style . . .

and a new one . . .

Golden Delicious . . .

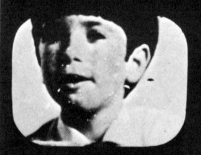

WOMAN: Very good, Tommy . . .

New Motts Golden Delicious Chunky with little chunks of golden delicious apple.

CHILD: And you thought Motts just made regular apple sauce . . .

Student Assignment

Student Assignment Number _____

Use the advertising/marketing information and objectives provided for the commercial on the preceding pages. Write a script and sketch the storyboard for a follow-up TV commercial in this campaign. Use the _____ structure.

Student Name:

Advertiser:

Title of Commercial:

Length of Commercial:

Video:

Audio:

Video:

Audio:

Video:

Audio:

Chapter 11

Television Guidelines: A Recapitulation

You'll find use for many of your talents when you create a TV commercial: the playwright's way with words, the artist's eye, the director's touch, the psychologist's understanding of what motivates people, the salesman's ambition to convince. Now, any one of these might tend to overbalance the others, so add your sense of judgment to obtain the proper equilibrium.

Your aim is to create a TV commercial with a powerful selling idea developed with imagination and presented with cohesiveness, unity, and structure. Another word for structure is form, and to aid you in your search for form here are some general guidelines. Not all of them are arbitrary, nor are they intended to stifle creativity; rather they should serve to keep you aware of the medium's advantages and limitations, and of the important target, the TV viewer you hope to convince.

1. Do your basic research first. Get the facts, all the facts you can about the product or service you are to advertise.

2. Analyze, then crystallize your research into major and minor selling points. Then focus on the strongest, most provocative possibility for a selling idea—and stress that one.

3. Your commercial must be relevant to the viewer's needs and wants. Make it meaningful to him in his terms.

4. Along with your native imagination and creativity, use taste, discretion, and respect for your viewer's intelligence.

5. The opening seconds of a spot are vital. These either grab and hold viewer attention or turn it off.

6. Don't overbuild: do not take too much time in the spot before you let the viewer know what is in it for him.

7. Whatever structure or technique you use for your commercial should be compatible with the product and the image you wish to project.

8. While you are developing the elements of your commercial, check back frequently with your copy platform. Stay on the track.

9. Television is primarily a visual medium, so your video directions should carry more than half the weight of your message.

10. Don't waste words. Make each one count. Keep them minimal. Use only as many as you really need.

11. Audio and video must relate to each other throughout the spot, or you'll confuse the viewer.

12. Avoid long, static scenes. Provide for movement of camera and/or actors.

13. Do not cram your spot with too many scenes or too much movement. How much is too much? That depends on the type of spot you are creating. A spot using the personality structure needs few scenes, a special effects spot could have many.

14. Don't expect to write a final script on the first try. True professionals rewrite and polish material through many revisions.

15. Which come first, words or pictures? That depends on your own creativity. Try it both ways. Try to visualize as you write.

16. Write your copy in a natural, conversational tone. Avoid the pretentious, the glib, the false.

17. Drawings for your storyboard can be simple ones. Stick figures will do for people.

18. One of the main reasons why the majority of TV commercials are ineffective is that the brand name has not been implanted strongly. People often recall a bit of action, perhaps the product category, but cannot single out the product. Identify your product clearly and forcefully.

19. Time your commercial. Read it aloud. Act it out. Don't rush it. A pace too fast for the viewer will leave him far behind.

20. Once you are satisfied with your script, set it aside. Become a devil's advocate. Look at the script later as objectively as you can. Examine it for impact, clarity, rhythm, pace, persuasion, relevance, and believability. If you do not score well, revise the script.

21. Video instructions and directions should be specific and exact.

22. If your product is new or has a new feature, give your spot an announcement flavor. TV viewers, like newspaper readers, appreciate and show more interest in something new.

23. Repetition can help register a selling idea. Don't expect the viewer to remember it if you say or show it only once in a 60-second spot.

24. Remember, your ad begins by going after attention. After that, it should involve people emotionally. Then it can convince—and sell.

25. At some point during the job of writing or sketching your storyboard you may think of other ways to do the commercial. One of them may be an improvement. If it is, start all over again with it.

Chapter 12

Institutional/Public Service Advertising

Every major corporation operates within the climate of public opinion. This climate can be restrictive or helpfully expansive. The use of institutional and public service advertising by manufacturers as a tool of public relations has increased considerably during recent years. It involves both commercial and non-commercial uses of advertising. In some instances, the purpose is to create a favorable impression and understanding for the advertiser and his policies rather than to promote directly the specific product he makes. Non-commercial advertising is usually concerned with the promotion of ideas and is most frequently used for reasons of public service or to influence public opinion.

Institutional advertising

Institutional advertising is used by the corporation to present itself as a forward-looking, progressive company of inherent strength and continuing vitality in order to foster a favorable climate in which to conduct its business. It does this by showing how the company contributes to an expanding economy. It reflects the philosophy, integrity, and quality standards of the company as expressed in scientific endeavors, management activities, and manufactured products.

When the institutional message is delivered as a television commercial, it often resembles a semi-documentary. It's not a true documentary because there usually has been considerable in-studio shooting involving the construction of costly sets. This kind of commercial is concerned with the broad objective of acquainting the public with the activities of the firm as it contributes to human welfare. So the commercial doesn't order the viewer out to his neighborhood store to buy a specific product. It stays away from hyperbole and bombast. It informs rather than exhorts, and the tone is almost always dignified, reserved, and restrained.

Institutional commercials are employed to enhance the reputation of and build good will for various groups—manufacturers, the military, an industry, service organizations, etc. The ads are used to inspire public esteem, confidence, and sometimes even affection for the group they represent.

Public service advertising

Public service advertising is a specific kind of institutional advertising, one which is concerned with improving the welfare of the American people. Public service advertising is designed to move ideas instead of products, to get something done which needs to be done, to support human needs and aspirations.

Public service advertising is handled principally through The Advertising Council, an organization which operates wholly on a voluntary basis. The Council is a private, non-profit organization of advertising, business and media people who have contributed billions of dollars in creative time and advertising to sell such things as better health, traffic safety, equal employment, education, forest fire prevention, and the United Nations.

Just to show the wide range of public service causes that can be furthered through television commercials of this nature, listed below are some of the many areas in which The Advertising Council has been the coordinator of promotional efforts.

- Educating the public on the importance of using seat belts in cars.
- Promoting forest fire prevention.
- Gaining public support of higher education.
- Promoting the "Religion in America" program.

On occasion, a manufacturer will conduct a public service campaign on its own. Shell Oil Co. during 1976 sponsored a series of "Bicentennial Minutes." By seeking to educate American television viewers to the events of 200 years ago, Shell contributed to the celebration of the Bicentennial, and earned itself much goodwill in the process.

Institutional commercials on television can and

do use most of the structures discussed earlier in this book—testimonial, demonstration, etc. Whichever structure is employed, the appeal is frequently to the emotions. This appeal is altogether logical when you consider that the subject matter deals with such sensitive areas as national and human resources. It is difficult (and illogical) to be unemotional about deaths caused by air pollution, or with the problem of keeping rodents away from children in squalid, rat-infested apartments.

Examples of institutional and public service television commercials follow.

INSTITUTIONAL MESSAGE
U.S. Navy—"Oceanography"

Objective:

To acquaint millions of Americans with the continuing research conducted by the U.S. Navy. In particular, to show how oceanographic research will help our country and its people.

Credits

Advertiser: U.S. Navy
Writer: Albert C. Book
Producer: David deVries
Director: Robert Gaffney

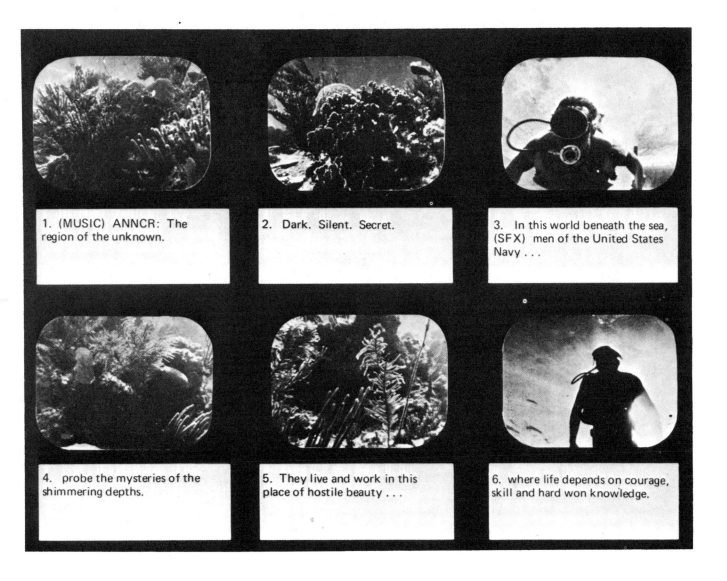

1. (MUSIC) ANNCR: The region of the unknown.

2. Dark. Silent. Secret.

3. In this world beneath the sea, (SFX) men of the United States Navy . . .

4. probe the mysteries of the shimmering depths.

5. They live and work in this place of hostile beauty . . .

6. where life depends on courage, skill and hard won knowledge.

7. Through their efforts the sea may some day release her long kept secrets.

8. Food for the earth's hungry millions.

9. Water to make deserts bloom.

10. All this and more will some day be a reality . . .

11. as the men of the United States Navy . . .

12. help unlock the secrets and wonders beneath the sea. (MUSIC UP AND OUT)

PUBLIC SERVICE MESSAGE

Urban Coalition Campaign—"Give a Damn"

Objective:

To create empathy in the white community for the problem of substandard housing in the ghetto.

Credits

Advertising agency: Young & Rubicam, Inc.
Writers: Bob Elgort and
Tony Isidore
Producer: Michael Ulick
Art director: Marv Lefkowitz

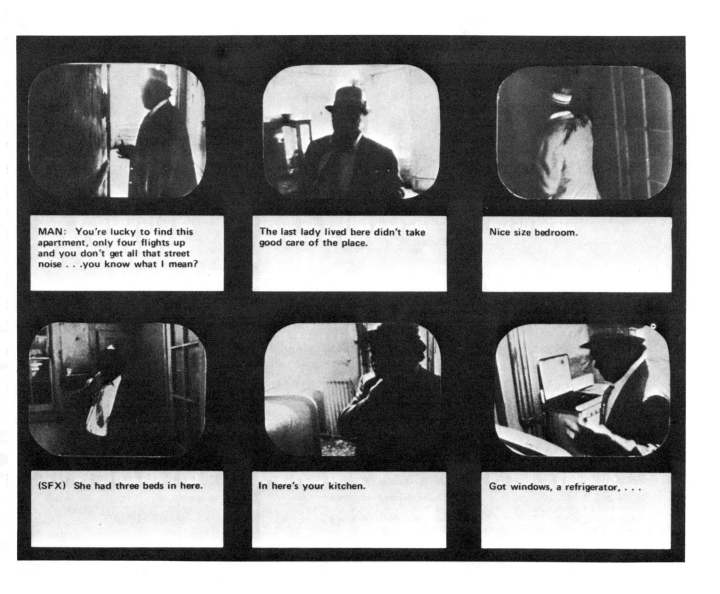

MAN: You're lucky to find this apartment, only four flights up and you don't get all that street noise . . .you know what I mean?

The last lady lived here didn't take good care of the place.

Nice size bedroom.

(SFX) She had three beds in here.

In here's your kitchen.

Got windows, a refrigerator, . . .

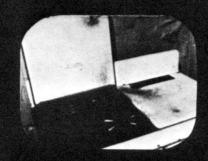

a good oven . . .

comes in handy when the weather turns cold.

And here's your bathroom.

(SFX)

A little 15 cent washer'll fix that up. You can get it in a hardware store.

Well that's it. Lots of people waiting to grab it so I got to know now. You want it or not?

New York Urban Coalition
Box 5100 G.C. Sta.
N.Y., N.Y. 10017

Give a damn

MAN: I'll take it. ANNCR: Almost half of all non-whites are forced to live in sub-standard housing . . .

You can help them through the New York Urban Coalition. Give jobs . . .Give money . . .

Give a damn.

Chapter 13
The Television Storyboard

A building contractor relies on the architect's specifications and blueprints. A commercial producer relies on a script and storyboard. Radio commercials require copy and descriptions of sound effects, music, and of how the copy is to be delivered. Television, because it is also visual, not only needs a script with all of radio's requirements, but also needs an artist's rendering of each scene. This rendering is called a "storyboard."

A storyboard's job

As you will note in your study of TV commercial structures in Chapter 10, each frame in the illustrations presents a continuation of some action, or a completely new scene, or an addition such as a super-imposed title. The illustrations in Chapter 10, however, are taken from the finished films, whereas actual storyboards are rendered in various degrees of "finish" in pencil, drawing pen, felt pen, wash, and sometimes photographs. When completed, storyboards show supervisors, clients, and commercial producers indications of the proposed action, types and extent of locations, sets, actors, special effects and titles.

A TV storyboard may consist of only one frame to show what will happen in a 10-second commercial, or dozens of frames to show what will happen in a spot lasting a minute or longer. Video and audio instructions are placed under each frame.

Within each frame, artwork or photography shows what the creator of the commercial has in mind—the setting and sequential action for each particular portion of the commercial.

The importance of a clear and understandable storyboard cannot be minimized. An easy-to-follow board will aid the evaluators in their approval or disapproval. A good idea with a good structure will show through even a poorly drawn board; conversely, a well-drawn board might also reveal the weakness of a lesser idea or a confusing structure.

Today, some storyboards are developed by individuals, and some by teams of two or more. Some

VIDEO: ECU OF LITTLE LEAGUER, SMILING, WAVING.

VIDEO: LS OF HOUSE. BOY ON BIKE PEDALS UP THE DRIVEWAY.

creators of commercials combine the talents of both writer and artist. Some advertising agencies have teams of writer/artist/producer who join talents to create a commercial. In this team effort, the writer can also suggest visual treatments and the artist can suggest copy. At its best, such teamwork stimulates free-wheeling creativity.

For your storyboard

For the purpose of using this book, let us assume that you will function as writer/artist. It is not important that you be a polished artist or even an adequate one. If you have little skill in drawing, stick figures will do very nicely; basic lines can indicate settings in the background. With even rudimentary skills you can indicate the scene, the number and types of people involved in each frame, and the proposed camera angles and focal distance—from closeup to long shot.

However crudely you draw the frames, your storyboard will permit you—and others—to "see" the sequential flow of your commercial, to judge its structure, cohesiveness, and continuity.

Storyboard development

In most agencies, a rough (basic) storyboard developed by a writer/artist will be reviewed by a producer (who advises on sets, techniques of camera work, and in-lab optical effects, etc.), by creative supervisors, and by account executives. It will then be sent, with corrections and changes, to the agency "bullpen." Here, the board will be drawn skillfully by sketchmen in a more comprehensive form.

Many people are involved in either creating or passing judgment on the storyboard. If they are imaginative, their suggestions, embellishments, and improvements will show up in the finished product.

When agency approval is won, the client's OK is sought. If granted, the commercial heads for production. The producer, director, and cameraman use the storyboard as a guide, a "blueprint," and bring their combined expertise to bear.

When creating your commercials and developing your storyboard, remember that television is a multi-sensory medium. It's sight and sound stimuli are designed to produce affirmative responses from prospective customers. Appeals to taste, touch, and smell (as in food, fabric, and coffee commercials) can be implied. Your script and storyboard should clearly indicate whatever appeals you use and the proposed degree in which you want them produced.

Chapter 14

The Length of TV Commercials

During the early days of commercial television the length of paid announcements varied from as short as 10 seconds to as long as nine minutes. Today, the 30-second spot is king. What brought about the change?

Several forces combined to bring about both change and order. In its infancy television was strictly a buyer's market. Agencies and advertisers willing to experiment in the new medium could pick and choose. Today, it's a seller's market.

The steadily rising costs of time and production worked to loosen and lessen sponsor's holds or "ownership" of time-slots and programs. Multi-participation is the keynote today, and all commercials are subject to more strictly enforced codes.

Another element should not be overlooked: researchers have discovered that a 30-second spot, effectively created, produced, and placed, will return as much as two-thirds the audience recall of a 60-second spot—at much less cost.

These forces have worked to ease out the 20-second spot almost entirely; and the emphasis has swung from 60s to 30s especially since 1968, according to the Bureau of Advertising Research.

Length of Television Spots (in percent)		
	1968	1977
Network 30-second	7	82
Network 60-second	44	6
Network other length	49	12
Non-network 30-second	12	81
Non-network 60-second	51	9
Non-network other length	37	10

If a commercial is to be one of a series on a sponsor's program or program segment (news, weather, etc.), it may well be a 60-second spot. If an advertiser has more than one product on the same program or program segment, you may create two 30-second spots and run them back to back. Or you might use 50 seconds to sell one product and use the final 10-second tag for another.

As the number of advertisers using television has increased, so has the number of commercials. NBC-TV changed the format of its 10 to 11 p.m. hour-long programs to provide fewer but longer commercial breaks. CBS-TV prime-time programs, since February 1976, have provided four 90-second breaks instead of its old six 60-second breaks.

Such practice has earned itself a name, "commercial clutter," and has caused more than a little consternation among agency and client media experts. Burke Copy Research discovered that from 25 to 40 percent of the TV audience will leave the room during these longer commercial breaks. And McCollum-Spielman, who also test commercials, have data that indicates a poorer performance, by 10 percent, for the middle spot in a three-commercial cluster.

What does this mean to media people intent on getting the most for each client dollar? They must evaluate available time slots and place spots to gain maximum cost-effectiveness. They must also work for a fair rotation when a spot becomes part of a cluster.

To creative personnel it means even more reliance on creating and crafting effectively, especially for a commercial for a national advertiser. The National Association of Broadcasters has, as part of its Code, a stipulation that large brand-name advertisers can sell only one product per commercial. No such restriction exists for local retail advertisers, and today these retail advertisers account for just about half of an average television station's revenue. This situation presents a major problem for both types of advertisers, and for the copywriters and art directors involved in making ads: how to stand out in a crowd.

Asking even a devoted never-leave-the-set viewer to recall copy points of three adjacent commercials is a tall order. So you, as creator of a commercial, must keep in mind the fact that your spot will doubtless be viewed along with at least two other spots much of the time. Don't overload your message with copy points.

One way advertisers cut down on costs is to create a 60-second spot and then edit a 30- or 20-second spot from the 60-second length. This allows for more flexibility in media planning. A spot buyer can shop for the best "rating points." These are determined by a complex estimate of the possible available audience and tuned-in audience at any one time.

The key question which has concerned the more sophisticated advertiser is, "To what extent, if any, is communication lessened in the shorter TV message?" The answer seems to be definite that in most cases the message can, indeed, accomplish its objective in the shorter time. This is based, of course, on the assumption that the abridgement is effectively done, that the prime selling theme stands out, that the shorter spot maintains a clear identity for the product or service.

In considering the possibility of using 20s or 30s over 60s the advertiser is primarily concerned with the establishment of the following:

1. **Viewer empathy**
   Does the degree to which viewers can see themselves in the situation depicted in the commercial vary according to commercial length?
2. **Viewer involvement**
   Does the ability of the commercial to attract and hold the viewer's attention vary according to the length of the commercial?
3. **Content communication**
   Does the content communication vary according to the length of the commercial?

The answers to these key points as culled from the efforts of research organizations, such as the TV Bureau of Advertising and the Schwerin Research Corp., indicate strongly that:

1. **Viewer empathy**
   Depends on execution rather than length of commercial. The shorter commercial is of sufficient length to develop empathy.
2. **Viewer involvement**
   Execution and/or content is the determining factor in viewer involvement, not whether the commercial is a 60- or 30-second version.
3. **Content communication**
   Communication varies only slightly between 60- and 30-second commercials.

In addition to the above conclusions, it is pertinent to note that in the area of brand recall the research organizations find that the shorter length commercial (30-second) delivers from 75 to 92 percent of the 60-second commercial level.

We may conclude from an analysis of relevant TV commercial research that the following key issues have been resolved:

1. Shorter commercials are generally better liked.
2. On the average, 30-second commercials register from 75 to 92 percent of the effectiveness of the 60-second commercial.
3. Longer commercials show optimum effectiveness up to 100 seconds, but beyond this point there is a definite fall-off.
4. An exceptional selling idea in a short spot can register more effectively than an average selling idea in a 60.

It follows that as you increase the length of a commercial, you do not get a proportionate increase of value as measured by recall, interest, believability, and similar indexes. It also follows that the not-so-secret ingredients of an effective TV commercial—be it an I.D., a 15-, 20-, 30-, 40-, 45-, or 60-second spot—are, first and last, creativity and craftsmanship.

Chapter 15

Research: Testing TV Commercials

By Patrick J. Kelly
Marketing Research Associates

The objective of any TV commercial testing service is to measure the ability of the commercial to sell, to be remembered, and to communicate. The need to know is accentuated by the size of the advertising budget invested in a campaign. With such a sizable investment at stake, it is advisable to know, beforehand, how a specific commercial will perform compared with another, either for the same product or for a competitor's product. The effectiveness of commercials varies widely.

To find out just where a specific commercial lies in the effectiveness spectrum, services have been established to uncover this information. Following are brief descriptions of some of the leading testing services—how they operate, what they offer.

Gallup & Robinson, Inc.

Gallup & Robinson's system of television commercial evauation provides three basic facilities: On-Air Syndicated Total Prime Time Television Research (TPT); On-Air Custom; and Theater Pre-Tests.

The research technique for the Total Prime Time (TPT) service is one of delayed, aided recall conducted via the telephone. The survey is based on interviews with approximately 3,300 men and women, 18 years of age and older, selected from telephone directories covering the Philadelphia area.

During the interview, last night's prime time program schedule is read and the interviewee is asked to reconstruct his viewing pattern by half-hour segments. All viewers exposed to brand-name cues selected from the viewer's total viewing pattern via a priority system that includes all client commercials, competitive commercials, and the necessary balance from an "all other" group.

Viewers claiming recall of any given commercial are asked a series of open-ended questions. The answers are recorded to determine proof of commercial registration (PCR), level of idea communication, and commercial persuasiveness. PCR scores are reported as a percentage of the available audience—men or women exposed to and asked about commercial exposure.

Because of increased participation and increased complexity in the development of TV marketing strategies, some advertisers need tailor-made measurements. In response to this need, Gallup & Robinson has developed a measurement on individual programs whenever, wherever, and with whomever the advertiser pleases.

The On-Air Single Show Surveys provide delayed, aided recall measurements using telephone interviewing. The service is available in 24 areas across the country, and additional markets can be added if needed. The basis reports developed are Proved Commercial Registration (PCR) and verbatim playback profiles leading to data on idea communication and buying attitudes.

For advertisers who want to pre-test commercials, an in-theater testing arrangement is available. A sample of respondents is invited to attend a theater to view a TV program. After viewing the program, they are questioned about the program and television in general—nothing is said about the commercial spliced into the film. The day following exposure, the respondents are interviewed by telephone to obtain recall levels and idea communication and favorable buying attitude effectiveness data.

Burke Marketing Research, Inc.

The Standard Burke Technique involves telephone interviews the day after the commercial was aired, using the aided recall method, and reflect normal in-the-home viewing situations.

The usual sample size is 200 viewers of the test program, which yields a Commercial Audience (those who were actually in the room with the set, not asleep and not changing channels at the time of the test commercial exposure) of approximately 150, varying slightly in either direction, depending on the type of program. Tests using other sample sizes can be arranged.

Respondents are those who claim to have watched the program on which the test commercial was telecast. Interviewing times are flexible, so that the interviewers can best reach the particular audience segment desired.

The following timetable is standard for most Burke day-after recall tests:

Flash scores, claimed and related recall, percentaged on Commercial Audience are reported by telephone during the morning of the day following the test. These rapidly computed scores are usually accurate within one or two percentage points, but are confirmed within about three more days. Friday, Saturday, and Sunday tests are flash-reported on the following Monday.

One hundred percent of the related and unrelated verbatims, coded and uncoded, can be available about five days after the date of interviewing. Final reports are available between three and four weeks from date of interviewing.

The standard report contains, basically, three items of decision-making information:
1. A quantitative measure of the communication's effectiveness.
2. A coded and categorized summary of all that was remembered about the commercial.
3. A verbatim transcription of the playback from every respondent recalling anything about the commercial.

Additionally, Burke maintains a file of normative data against which recall scores for a specific study may be compared. Current normative data show mean averages, ranges, and bar graph distributions of claimed and related scores by length of commercial, product category, and by sex.

Schwerin Research Corp.

Central to the Schwerin Research Corp. system is the assumption that advertising's ability to persuade consumers to prefer a given brand over its competition is the key indicator of effectiveness. Based on this assumption, several measures have been developed to reflect this position.

The Standard Service includes the Competitive Preference Score, Persuasibility Index, Brand Identification (Unaided), and Unaided Recall and Involvement. To supplement the basic standard measure, Schwerin Research has developed a variety of "diagnostic" measurements which are used to assist in understanding the influence underlying advertising effectiveness—the Extended Service.

The technique used by Schwerin to measure the effectiveness of television advertising centers on a test audience in a test theater. A randomly selected panel is subjected to viewing a "pilot" TV film

throughout which are interspersed some TV commercials.

The test audience is selected from telephone directories covering the geographical area surrounding a particular test center. Although the total audience on a given night represents a cross-section of the population 16 years of age or older and test data are obtained from the entire audience, the sample may be redefined after the fact so that test results for a particular product are based only on relevant consumers—namely the analytical sample.

Following the introductory warm-up during which the test director outlines the purpose of the session and gives specific procedural instructions—but before any exposure to a stimulus of any kind has taken place—the audience is offered the chance to win some prizes. In order to qualify for a prize, every respondent is asked to complete a ballot by checking the particular brand of which he would like to receive a quantity as a prize. Several product categories are included and within each are listed the principal competing brands. Tickets are drawn on stage and the winner is given a specified amount of the product he selected in a given category. This technique may be regarded as a simulation of real buying behavior and ultimately provides data for the "Pre-Choice Measurement."

The audience is then shown the pilot program and three commercials (for one of the brands in each of the "Pre-Choice" checklists). The same pilot program is repeated from session to session to eliminate this element as a variable.

At the conclusion of the program, measures of "Unaided Recall" and "Brand Identification" are obtained, followed by the "Post-Choice Measurement," which is developed in the same manner as the "Pre-Choice" brand selections and drawings.

Summarization of the brand selections made after exposure to the test advertisement provides data for the "Post-Choice" percentages, which reflect the proportions of consumers favorably disposed toward brands in the respective product fields, after exposure to a commercial for a brand in that field. The "Post-Choice" information serves as the final ingredient for the over-all effectiveness measure.

Next, the involvement measure is obtained followed by a short audience discussion about the program. For Extended Service Tests the advertisement is again shown—out of program context—allowing for the special diagnostic questioning.

AdTel, Ltd.

The AdTel technique uses a dual-cable CATV system and two balanced purchase diary panels of 1,200 households each. The system has been wired using two cables, thus permitting wiring of panel homes to either cable to provide an alternate A and B checkerboard distribution.

AdTel can cut in test commercials to the B homes, while the A homes continue to get normal ad exposure. The corporate client must own the time—network or spot—into which the test commercial is cut. A client can have an unlimited number of cut-ins made without paying any cut-in charge.

Two matched panels are maintained—one for each cable. Panel families are personally recruited and trained. They must record all the food, drug, and other appropriate purchases in a weekly diary.

In addition to purchase information, the diary contains a symptom section which enables AdTel to measure low-incidence health care products based on usage. A household reports the number of times each brand was taken by family members for various symptoms—headache, stomach ache, cold, cough, etc. This information makes it possible for a manufacturer to test a campaign against a specific usage.

Panel members receive points for completing their weekly diaries. These points are redeemable for merchandise from a well-known mail-order catalog. These, together with other incentives, total about $100 a year for the consistent but average housewife.

To substantiate the written reports, AdTel conducts quarterly pantry and medicine chest audits. These records are compared by computer against diary-reported purchases. This follow-up check helps to impress panelists that AdTel wants complete and accurate diary entries.

Data from the purchase diaries are processed into a four-week report. For each brand specified by the client, shares of unduplicated families purchasing, units, dollars, volume in ounces or another common denominator, and percentage of deal volume are shown.

In addition, a client receives a raw deck of data cards (or tape) covering every diary-recorded transaction in the product categories desired. These data enable the client to track such factors as trial and repeat, brand switching, the demographics of triers, users, and switchers, the importance of dealing, etc.

AdTel also conducts three attitude and awareness studies throughout the year among people on the cable but not on the panel. These studies are intended to be diagnostic rather than definitive and can be helpful in guiding analysis of the diary panel data.

Milwaukee Advertising Laboratory

The Milwaukee Advertising Laboratory is a research facility that provides a set of controlled conditions in a natural setting, within which the sales effectiveness of newspaper, Sunday supplement, direct mail, and television advertising can be measured without disturbing a current marketing program.

Two matched markets were developed by taking the four counties comprising the Greater Milwaukee Market and dividing them into 104 newspaper circulation districts with about 2,500 newspaper subscribers in each. These were then split into two equal and matched markets of 52 districts each. From these two markets, probability samples of 750 families each are drawn.

Newspaper advertising reaching these two matching markets is controlled on a split-run and split distribution basis. Television advertising is controlled through the use of an electronic muter which is installed in all of the TV sets of the two samples. With the muter in use, it is possible to blank out a set of commercials from one group while the other group receives the message. The television set simply goes blank, as does the sound, for the interim of the commercial but then returns to "live" for the program.

To collect the needed information, the Laboratory makes use of a consumer purchase diary. Each homemaker in each sample is asked to send in a weekly diary of all branded merchandise bought during the week. She is given instructions on how to do this during a basic placement interview.

To compensate the homemaker for her cooperation, the Laboratory provides free maintenance service on all TV sets in the household for the duration of the householder's participation as a panel member. Also, she can earn merchandise prizes from points earned by continued cooperation.

The weekly diaries are processed by computer, and printouts are sent directly to subscribing advertisers and their agencies. The reports show the total number of units bought in the product category, the distribution of brand shares by units, and the percentage in each market separately. Parallel reports cover dollar sales in total and by brands, the volume of sales in total and by brands, and additional data on the extent dealing affects volume each month.

Commercial Testing Service

Two types of measurements to appraise the performance of television commercials are offered by Commercial Testing Service: an evaluative measure and a diagnostic measure.

The evaluative measures are related to how well the commercial succeeds in building consumer acceptance and interest in the advertised brand. In addition to the over-all measure of the effectiveness, CTS also offers measures defined by demographic characteristics (age, education, etc.), by product usage characteristics (heavy versus light users), and by brand attitude or brand usage segments.

The diagnostic measures are designed to appraise the content and execution of the commercial, including analysis of the points communicated, the extent to which the commercial message is considered important, believable, interesting, or involving.

Invitations to serve on a panel are mailed to

residents living within a four- to six-mile radius of a suburban theater where the research session will be held. The invitation offers an opportunity to express opinions on television programs and commercials and states that door prizes will be awarded along with additional incentives for attendance and cooperation.

The testing procedure is as follows: Respondents are given a questionnaire in which they rate a number of brands in a number of product categories, using a five-point attitude scale. They are then shown a film which they are told is being considered for TV. Within the film are four commercials for non-competing prands in some but not all of the product categories for which they had previously indicated brand ratings. After the screening, the respondents are given a second questionnaire with several questions about the film. Then they are told that there will be a series of drawings and the prizes will be a specified number of units of the product. They are asked to indicate how many of each of a restricted list of competitive brands they would like to win if their name is drawn. Obviously, the respondent would tend to indicate more of the brand most preferred.

A third questionnaire contains, for each commercial, a number of open-ended questions designed to provide information used in the diagnostic tabulation. It is also possible to include questions of the client's own design in this questionnaire.

The principal measure provided shows the gain or loss in buying interest caused by advertising exposure. Respondent attitude toward the various brands is predicated on the number of each brand indicated in the prize-drawing procedure. This ranking compared with the attitude recorded prior to test advertising indicates the effectiveness of the commercial.

Chapter 16

Producing the TV Commercial

You have created a commercial. Its selling idea is firmly locked into your storyboard. You have obtained approval within the agency and from the client. The budget has been approved. This is the go-ahead sign for production. And you see, perhaps reluctantly, the producer take over.

Ideally, you have worked closely with the producer in the creation of the commercial. During this time, he has assisted and guided you with his imagination and technical expertise. From now on he is in charge, and you will assist and guide him.

The producer's role

Some producers work for film production firms; some are strictly free-lance; but for our example, the producer will be on staff at an agency. What does he do?

First, we should assume that the producer really knows the ins and outs of film, tape, and live media. Completely. Given that knowledge as a base, he works from two points of view: creative and practical. He contributes his creativity to helping bring about an imaginative, professional, selling message. At the same time he works within the production budget, keeps production moving ahead, and is the hub around which a dozen or more phases of filmmaking act like spokes of a wheel. He combines his artistic and business sense under one hat, because only a smooth combination of these polarized talents will help make an effective commercial.

The producer takes the storyboard and has several copies of it made. He sends these to film production houses for bids, houses selected from a long list as best qualified for this particular type of commercial. The number of bids varies. Some agencies and clients insist on as many as five bids. Others settle for three. Still others, having had an agreeable experience with a particular firm's work in the past, may opt for that house—if the price is right.

Film houses can generalize or have specialties. Animation may be one firm's forte, unusual type-

photography may be another's. The producer takes this into consideration when he sends the storyboard out for bids. He also considers each firm's past performance, current output, adherence to shooting schedules, production talent, and ability to deliver quality prints on time.

When the selection has been made, a contract is drawn up between the agency (acting in behalf of the client) and the production house. Nothing is left to chance or to memory. A commercial represents a big investment for the client and production costs go up each year. In the past 10 years, the increase ranges from 150 to 200 percent.

Pre-production meeting

Businessmen seem to find all kinds of excuses for holding meetings, but there is a good reason behind the pre-production conference: it is a meeting of minds. It is attended by the production house representatives (including their producer and director, if possible), the writer, the art director, and is chaired by the agency producer. Some clients like to attend to be reassured that their objectives are being met.

At this meeting the storyboard is reviewed frame by frame, sequence by sequence. The objective is kept clearly in mind, and all suggestions and refinements are focused on the job of meeting the objective of the commercial. Ideas are exchanged on sets, actors, sound effects, music—every facet of the spot. Agreement and understanding are reached, a shooting schedule is planned, and the production house goes to work. They set aside studio time for the filming and arrange for the crew. If locations are indicated in the storyboard, they arrange for a scouting date, one the agency producer can make.

In production

From this meeting on, the agency producer is in day-to-day contact with the production firm. The details are multitudinous. Sets must be designed and the sketches approved. Props must be gathered, ordered, or built, and approved. Costumes must be agreed upon. The director selects his cameraman, unless this has already been done. Art work and titles are executed and approved. Not even the smallest detail should go unplanned.

Auditions are held for whatever actors are needed. If a new announcer is to be used, auditions are held for that job. (The casting procedure is developed at length in a later section.)

Shooting date

Your commercial is to be filmed on a studio sound stage. Last-minute preparation is evident from very early in the morning. Final touches are given to the set, and the property master arranges the props (including duplicates and triplicates in case of breakage or soilage).

The agency producer is the voice of authority on the set. He works closely with the production house team, constantly consulting with director, cameraman, and crew chiefs. Lighting is set for the first scene. Actors rehearse, get their makeup, rehearse some more. And after much coffee and prune danish, the assistant director calls for quiet on the set and the director goes for Take One, Scene One.

As the creator of this commercial, you are in evidence. You observe. You comment—but to the agency producer. He will relay your observations and suggestions to the director. You may wonder if a piece of business may be acted differently to get a better effect. You may question an on-camera reading, or prefer a tighter close-up of the product than the director has set up.

The more you learn about film production, the more valuable your suggestions will become, and, consequently, the more experience you will bring to your next creative assignment.

Take follows take, scene follows scene. Often, the pace seems snail-like, but professionalism includes a large dose of patience. Use it. And finally, after a good take on the last scene, the order is given to print it and the filming portion of this production is wrapped up.

Sound and music

Your commercial may require that the sound track be recorded simultaneously with the filming, especially if actors are involved in a problem-solution structure. Or, if your commercial calls for an announcer voiceover, chances are good that the producer will tape the audio track before the studio date.

At this taping session, held in a sound sudio, the announcer and/or actors work with the script, rehearsing it under the direction of the agency producer. Sound experts monitor the voice levels, adjust microphones for position, and keep a log of the takes. The length of the session depends on the complexity of your commercial and the talents of your announcer and actors. At this session the writer contributes suggestions as to inflections, emphasis, pacing, etc. He is sometimes asked to rewrite a sequence that may be awkward to read. A writer can often improve a commercial in the recording studio, just as he can at the actual filming, by constantly being alert to the possibilities of enhancing the commercial's communicability—or, in plain English, by making the persuasion and sell come through.

Music and sound effects may be recorded at this session or at separate sessions. Recording tape gives a producer flexibility. He can record voice, sound effects, or music on separate tracks. If the music has been selected from "stock"—a large bank of music and musical effects that is readily available in large cities—that music is transferred to tape. If musicians and singers are used, this recording session is set up and conducted in a manner similar to the announcer's.

At last, the producer has, say, three tapes: announcer, music, and sound effects. They are transferred to 35mm magnetic tape. The producer then arranges for a mix. At a sound studio with multi-track facilities, the three tapes are placed on separate reels, synchronized for time, and run. The sound engineer "mixes" the tracks together, combines them, each with its own level of volume. The result is a single track with all the sound combined, each at the proper level and intensity.

Going for approval

Being able to juggle might help any would-be producer. Many things have to be done, and all at just about the same time.

Generally, the day following the shooting date sees the appearance of the "dailies." These are the takes that met on-set approval for printing.

The producer notes the clack-board number of each preferred take, and these are pulled out of the master reel. Edited together, they become the work print. There are no dissolves or titles in this print. It is for viewing, for re-editing work, and for approvals. These latter are obtained at an interlock session; the film is run through one projector, the sound track is played through another in sync. Additional changes may be suggested. From this point to finish, however, changes are more involved and more costly that changes up to this point.

When approvals are given on the work print, the producer and the film editor pull out the original (and, you hope, still unscratched) footage. In the film laboratory, each sequence is assembled in order and combined with any special effects footage, titles, etc. Cuts or dissolves are incorporated into the film where directed. The sound track is physically incorporated onto the resultant film, producing the answer print.

Again, approvals are needed. Proper color or

tonal values are checked, and if found wanting, noted. Smoothness and length of dissolves are also checked. Once again the lab goes to work and comes out with a corrected answer print. Given its approval, the lab produces the final, correct, perfect release print.

After final OK

The producer's job is almost over. And so is yours, as creator, at least for this commercial. Prints for on-air use are ordered, received, checked out carefully for quality, and sent to whatever TV stations are on the media schedule.

All the foregoing is, of necessity, but a summary of events in the production life of a commercial. Details would fill a book at least the length of this one. But the summary should give you some indication of the enormous attention to detail, as well as the combination of creativity and craftsmanship, that goes into a TV commercial. The constant, meticulous attention that so many people put into a commercial helps to make it effective as a selling tool.

The production of a commercial can take as long as three months or even longer. No corner can be cut, no slice of time saved, without some loss to the commercial. Some commercials are completed in a few days or weeks, but this is never easy and can be risky. It is also expensive; but expense can be justified if a client is rushing a TV spot to a special market in which he is testing or introducing a new product.

But time, long or short, is not the answer in making an effective commercial. Work is. Creativity and craftsmanship are evidenced and reflected in every television spot that attracts attention, involves the viewer, offers conviction, persuades—and sells.

Television stations transmit program and commercial material originating live or material that has been recorded on film or videotape. (Slides are not a major factor.) Each source has its advantages and limitations. In the following sections we will summarize the qualities, benefits, and drawbacks of each type.

FILM

By any measure, film is the most versatile, flexible, and widely used medium for TV spot production. Studios in major cities have complete facilities for photographing the most complex commercials. Studios range in size from small "insert" rooms used exclusively for close-up work (of packages, hands, labels, etc.) to animation studios where drawings are photographed frame by frame, to the huge, arena-like sound stages in the Los Angeles, California, area. Most of the latter belong to major feature-film studios which often devote a large portion of their production schedules to the filming of TV programs and spots.

Reliable, creative production houses either have their own studios or rent space when filming a commercial. These companies can be found in Canada, Mexico, Puerto Rico, and throughout Europe. Just as Hollywood is no longer the only center for feature films, it and New York City are no longer the only centers for the production of spots for television. Many agencies and clients use European studios for special scenes or special casting, not to mention production economies. Because the production field is extremely competitive, there is practically no limit to the effects you can ask for and get on film—budget willing.

Location shooting

More and more, commercials are being filmed on location. And for many good reasons. Improvement in film quality, fast jet travel, wider use of off-beat camera techniques, and the compelling desire to look different from competition are some. But the overriding reason is authenticity or realism. For many commercials today, this demand practically necessitates location shooting—even multi-location shooting is required in some cases.

For talent, production crew, and agency and client personnel to go on location, the budget must be generous and the objectives worthwhile. Location shooting is costly, but it must be weighed against achieving (or trying to achieve) authenticity in a studio. Because of feature films and their colorful, authentic locales, viewers have grown accustomed to realism. And this quality in a commercial can add to the spot's believability.

Commercials for spaghetti are now filmed in Italy, the coffee tree areas of Colombia are familiar TV sights and Paris is a much-used backdrop for fashion and perfume spots. Airlines with overseas routes enhance their images by spotlighting foreign scenes. Pipe tobacco spots are photographed on ski jumps and fresh-orange-juice commercials are shot on Florida beaches. All these locations are used for the realism they bring to the commercials.

As we have stated, motion pictures are, in part, responsible for this trend. Another stimulus has come through the flexibility of TV news programs whose cameramen and reporters are all over the world. On-the-spot reports are filed every day and funneled into every TV home as a matter of course. Again, viewers have come to accept, even expect, location shots from anywhere in the world.

Be guided by your objectives in deciding between studio and location. If location shooting will give you a more authentic-looking commercial for your product, make it show up on your storyboard. Perhaps you need a location only to set the stage for your message. If this is the case, your producer can obtain footage already in existence from a stock film company. Then you can shoot the balance of your commercial in close-ups in a studio—and save.

The film

Your commercial structure and content will dictate and determine studio versus location filming. It will also influence your producer and director in their choice of film size and color. Almost no commercials are filmed in black and white today; color is king. The reasoning is simple: color TV set owners expect to see color. Color production is more expensive than black and white, but the extra dimension of realism it gives a commercial is considered well worth it.

The quality of color film has improved enormously over the years. Tones, shading, and light values can be controlled to a fine degree. Experimentation has widened the range of effects available and made color film an artistic medium of expression.

In 1977, it was estimated that half of filmed commercials were shot in 35mm and half in 16mm film. For broadcast, national spots for network use are normally submitted in 35mm form along with two 16mm reduction prints. The 35mm film is transferred to videotape for airing, and the 16mm prints are used as security backups. Most local television stations require spots to be submitted as 16mm prints.

By carefully planning each scene, your director will include everything you want inside the safety area, the portion of film frame surrounded by the TV cut-off zone. This zone is the area around the perimeter of the TV receiver that does not show the outer portions of each frame of film. Everything inside its circumference will be seen on a TV receiver. And within this area, of course, your action and titles will be placed. Perhaps you have been made aware of this while viewing some old feature film that had titles stretched across the screen. These would all be seen in a theater, but the letters far left and far right are cut off on your home TV screen.

Sixteen millimeter production

The narrower, smaller, 16mm frame is becoming more popular with amateur movie makers. It is also used for reports on many TV news programs.

Sixteen millimeter film is easier to work with than 35mm, and the cameras for 16mm are lighter and more mobile. The film can be less expensive to develop and to edit. But it has some restrictions. Fewer special effects are possible. You have less control over grain, color quality and total values. When 16mm is transferred to video tape or blown up to 35mm, it loses an appreciable percentage of pictorial clarity and intensity; it becomes less sharp.

However, 16mm is ideal for some commercials. Today, some spots are filmed in 16mm to achieve a reportorial, or *cinema-verite* quality. Hand-held cameras move, bounce, pan quickly, zoom in and out. Directors use this technique to gain and transmit a feeling of actuality, of realism and spontaneity. It can be extremely effective, all other facets of the commercial being equal.

Costs

Film commercials can be costly, and indeed, most often are. Today, $150,000 spots are not at all uncommon. A few, a very few, cost even more. Because production costs include so many variables, a true average would not be meaningful. The average range, however, is between $14,000 and $35,000 for a 60-second color commercial.

A recent study by the American Association of Advertising Agencies showed that a $10,000 b&w film commercial in 1963 cost $17,200 in color in 1968. That same color commercial in 1978 might cost $40,000. Charges for everything continue to rise.

On the following page is a cost breakdown of a typical commercial production. It suggests, if nothing else, that the commercial creator is responsible for making every client dollar do its job. And that job is to sell.

To sum up

Film is flexible, versatile, colorful. It can give a viewer breathtaking tones and almost no end of special lighting effects and techniques. In the camera, or at the laboratory where film is processed, or at the editing bench, experts can bring many dazzling effects into being: fancy opticals, wipes, dissolves, overlaps, fractionalized or split screen units, prism shots, flash cuts, slow and fast motion—the list is almost endless.

You can take and retake sequences then select the ones best qualified for your film. You can zero in on extreme microphotography. You can, as one golf ball spot did, start on a close-up of the ball and zoom back for what seems like half a mile. You can use a narrow field of vision or a wide-angle lens. You can also pan, truck, go out of focus or come into focus. In the commercials that you create, you are limited only by your knowledge and imagination, your production staff's ingenuity, and, of course, by your client's time and money.

TAPE

Video tape is no longer the coming thing. It is here. Ninety percent of network daytime and 65 percent of nighttime television is on tape. Nearly all TV stations serving American markets are equipped with video tape facilities. With the exception of sports events, news, and weather shows, tape has replaced film and live as a vehicle for programs. But tape lags behind film for spot use.

Tape advantages

The proponents of video tape argue that it has three basic advantages over film: A more brilliant, clearer picture and sound, a shorter production time, and more control in the studio—you can see what you're doing each step of the way.

Estimated Cost of Producing One 60-second Television Commercial
in 35mm Color Film
1977

Studio Rental	$ 1,333	**Equipment**	
		Camera, Lights, Sound	590
Preparation		**Miscellaneous**	
Director, Assistant Director (one day)	665	Insurance, Shipping, Inspecting, etc.	565
Set Preparation		**Film & Processing**	2,187
Crew costs (one day each)		**Lettering, Animation, Opticals**	1,330
Scenic Designer	232	**Editing**	
Scenic Artist	123	Supervising Editor, Editor, Assistant	
Scenic Artist, Journeyman	87	Editor, and Projectionist	530
Chief Carpenter	120	**Re-Recording & Mixing**	
Second Carpenter	87	Sound Track—Outside	590
Chief Grip	100		
Second Grip	87	**Subtotal**	13,089
Chief Prop—Inside	100		
Chief Prop—Outside	100	**Production House Fee**	5,300
Chief Electrician	100		
Assistant Director	135	**Production House Total**	18,389
Pension & Welfare	195		
Shooting Crew		**Talent**	
Producer	400	Three On-Camera	616
Director (Staff)	325	One Voice-Over	162
Assistant Director	165	(Includes Pension & Welfare)	
Script Clerk	87	**Music**	
Scenic Designer	165	Copy & Arrange	2,325
Cameraman	325	Pension & Welfare	33
Assistant Cameraman	240	**Recording**	
Chief Electrician	125	Studio & Materials	365
Assistant Electrician	110	**Photostats**	96
Scenic Artist	110	**Photoscripts**	35
Chief Grip	110	**Production Visuals**	325
Second Grip	103	**Wardrobe**	100
Chief Prop	125		
Second Prop	110	**Total Costs**	22,446
Sound Boom Man	95	**Agency Commission (15%)**	3,366
Sound Recordist	95		
Sound Mixer	125	**Total Cost Estimate for Commercial**	$25,812
Makeup Artist	103		
Hairdresser	110		
Wardrobe	83		
Pension & Welfare	412		
Striking			
One Prop, One Electrician, One Grip			
(Including Pension & Welfare)	310		

Most people are unable to distinguish between a live telecast and one on video tape. Tape records electronically and plays back electronically for transmission; there is no perceptible loss of quality. Tape gives commercials a sense of "presence" which is important to advertisers.

Speed is all-important to advertiser and agency. Tape is immediate, it requires no processing, whereas film must be developed, printed and copied before it can be edited. A tape commercial can be completed in hours, whereas film can take weeks.

Tape also allows the entire production team to view "takes" immediately, make suggestions and improvements, and retake and view again. Re-shooting with film means re-renting studio and equipment, and calling back crew and performers.

Until recently, editing of video tape was a special problem, but innovations have given producers a broader range of effects. Advanced taping facilities include a system which permits exact frame-by-frame editing. Your commercials can include flash cut editing, time lapse sequences, moving mats (e.g., a miniature human figure relating to giant size products or vice versa; a man sliding through the sky and landing in a car; titles that zoom off or onto packages; a variety of wipes, etc.).

With so much going for it, you might wonder why tape is not used for all commercials, but tape does have its limitations. Out-of-the-way location shooting, full-cell animation, fast motion or slow motion can be best achieved with film.

Copies of video tape commercials generally cost more than film prints. Time, and a greater use of tape in the future, may help equalize this, especially as more tape facilities, studio and mobile, become available.

Creating tape spots

If your commercial is to be taped, you create it with tape's advantages and limitations in mind. The producer plans his pre-production just as carefully for tape as he does for film. On the day(s) of the taping, he constantly checks with the director, cameraman, set designer, light technician, etc.

After each good take, everyone concerned can watch the monitor and decide on retakes.

When every segment of the commercial is taped, whatever editing has not already been completed in the camera or control room (wipes, dissolves, etc.) can be started almost immediately. If sound was recorded simultaneously with the picture, the finished commercial can be ready for copying and be on the air in a matter of hours.

LIVE

Live commercials were the rule in the early days of television, even for network shows. From simplistic announcer-on-camera-holding-the-product, to e-laborate studio productions, live commercials, telecast as they were being performed, were exciting, frustrating, dull, and sometimes excruciating.

Every nuance, every light, every piece of business, props, letter-perfect actors—every detail of a live commercial had to be preplanned and rehearsed. The comic history of television includes commercials that featured refrigerator doors that wouldn't open, dogs that refused pet food, cleansers that failed to wipe up dirt. No wonder film became the major medium for commercials!

Relatively few commercials are done live today. And most of these are on local TV stations' news and personality shows. Some network "talk-and-plug-my-latest-movie" shows have the host or announcer deliver the commercial, but these are the exception rather than the rule.

Creating a commercial for live delivery demands simplicity, first because your set will be restricting. They will generally have one camera—two, if you're lucky. So you must plan your moves, dissolves, and cuts carefully, allowing time for changing a lens or repositioning a camera. And you cannot expect to have carte blanche in sets or lighting or talent.

Whatever titles you use may be artwork, used directly on camera, or translated into slides and fed into the system on cue by the director.

Production

The producer will take your finished and approved script and list everything needed. He'll have a conference with the TV station's production manager as well as the show's producer and director. (At smaller TV stations these may be one and the same person.) Once the talent is cast, the props gathered, and the artwork completed, rehearsal time is set up. This usually takes place immediately prior to the actual show.

Because time in the studio is so valuable, your producer and the show's director will work fast. Camera moves will be plotted and written on the script. (Station directors seem to prefer this practice to the use of storyboards, although they will consult your board and often make suggestions.) Everyone involved learns his commercial cues. The technical director (responsible for picture quality), the sound engineer, the cameraman, the floor manager, and the director all work as a team to give your commercial professional smoothness and pace.

CASTING

Let us assume that you have created a commercial. The storyboard has been approved and the budget has been signed. How do you and your producer make sure that your commercial will have spontaneity and vitality before you go to the studio to film it? By selecting your actors and announcer with care.

Announcers should be chosen for their voice qualities and the expressive way they read the copy. Actors should be chosen because they best express the characters in the commercial, not because they are fashion-model pretty or handsome. An actor's projection of character, his presence, is the quality to look for. Commercials must involve the viewer emotionally in order to create conviction—and sales. An actor must have conviction himself and express it in a spontaneous manner.

Casting directors

If you work in a small advertising agency, you and your producer will probably do the casting. Large agencies have casting directors on their staffs, usually persons with theatrical experience and entertainment world contacts.

It is absolutely essential that the casting director know precisely the mood and tone of your commercial as well as its objective. Explain your thoughts about the commercial as you discuss the storyboard.

Your casting director will have files on all available actors and announcers, with pictures and lists of credits (plays, movies, and commercials that each actor has done). You'll save time by going through the pictures the casting director selects before audition time. But be careful: some of the pictures may have been taken and retouched years ago.

Auditions

The casting director will then call the actor through his agent and schedule a time spot for an audition. Time can be saved by scheduling actors to appear in 10-minute intervals at the audition room (a large one in your office or at the production house). Fifteen minutes is a more comfortable time allotment for announcers. This will give them the opportunity to go over the script by themselves in the outer waiting room. Also, give them time during the audition to change or alter their reading to gain the special emphasis you want.

You should have a list of the people who will audition, with enough space on the page to write your comments about their audition performance.

When the talent appears and introductions are made, try to put the actor at ease. Even long-time professionals sometimes become nervous at auditions. After a general comment or two, describe the product you are advertising, the commercial, and the specific character you want him to audition for. Give him a few moments to go over the storyboard or script. Then let him read his part aloud, perhaps twice if he's on the right note. Give him any suggestions, but do not correct him with a reading of your own. Remember, you are hiring a professional who, with direction at rehearsal and on the set, will give his

best characterization. Chances are, he'll come through with a reading that has nuances that you had not known were in the script.

If your commercial has two or more actors with dialogue, audition them together so that you can note stature, mannerisms, and interactions. Write your comments before the next actor or group of actors come into the room to audition. It will be a helpful jog to your memory in later discussions.

Don't waste time, yours or the actor's. Two or three readings should be enough to indicate an actor's proficiency and suitability. And contrary to some Broadway producers' opinions, actors are human beings. Be courteous. Friendly, but professional. This will help build a good attitude on the set when you film your spot.

On the air

When commercial time is reached, this team repeats its directions, camera moves, and action. The director in his sound-proof booth calls instructions to cameramen, sound and picture engineers. The talent on camera performs. The hours and days of creating, writing, and producing are centered in these relatively few seconds. Almost before you know it, your commercial is over, the show is resumed.

To sum

Live commercials call for a lot of hard work, but they have their advantages. Shopping specials for supermarkets and department stores are timely. Spots for automobiles, for example, are given an immediacy, a "news" quality. Live commercials are relatively inexpensive and are easier to write, set up, and produce than filmed or taped spots. Live commercials also can be produced much faster and more economically.

Video tape

Some agencies have video-tape systems. These can be valuable to you when you cast a commercial. A taped audition is by no means a finished, polished example of an actor's or announcer's work, but it will give you an on-the-spot indication of how well he will perform in your commercial. It will do two more things: taping can facilitate post-audition reviews with the producer and possibly the client; and the reel of tape can be placed in the agency's archives as part of a growing record of a pool of talent for reference in future casting sessions.

"Real" people

Perhaps your commercial is a testimonial which involves actual housewives, mechanics, etc., rather than professional actors. Where do you find them? The fast and easy way is to keep a "lookout" at your product's point of purchase. Make note of each customer. A short interview with selected ones should tell you if you have a potential user-spokesman for your product. Plan to invite your two top choices to the studio—just in case one "freezes" once the camera is turned on.

Talent payment

Paying for the talent is the responsibility of the agency casting director and/or producer, but as a creator of commercials, you should know the varying scales. Talent payment and repayment (residuals) can add up to a large part of any commercial's budget. Obviously, 20 men and women, all on camera, all with lines, will be far more costly than two characters who have no lines. It is part of your job to know your talent costs before you go over budget at the storyboard stage.

The Screen Actors Guild (SAG) represents actors who appear in filmed or taped commercials. The American Federation of Television and Radio Artists (AFTRA) is another union to which commercial performers belong. Definite rates or scales of pay have been set for differing appearances in commercials. Actors appearing in spots shown on coast-to-coast networks receive more money than, say, an actor in a commercial shown only in a small local area. An actor who appears as a principal character in a spot receives more pay than another actor in the same spot who appears only as an "extra."

It is not necessary to detail here the multitude of pay scales. Let us rather sum up with this guideline: in these cost-conscious times, it is not only an economic necessity but also an imaginative creative practice to keep the number of actors in your commercials within the bounds of the budget.

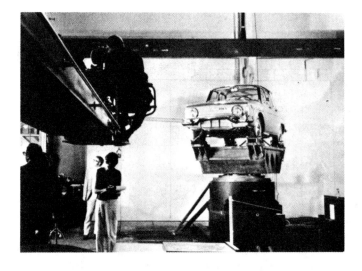

In this photo taken in a production studio, a Renault car is set atop a vibrating machine to undergo the punishment of 3,300 lbs. of vibrating force, as part of a "demonstration" commercial.

Chapter 17
Creative TV Assignments

"MASTER"

As an exercise in creativity, here is an opportunity to plan and prepare a commercial without an actual one of the same type as a guide or idea starter. All of the pertinent details concerning the nature and purpose of, and the market for, the product for which you are to create the commercial are given below. The specific nature of the suggested commercial in this particular case is outlined here under "Assignment." The product is a hypothetical one and the name is fictitious. It is called "Master," and is a hair preparation for men.

Background information

Product: A spray-on hair groom for men. Non-greasy. Especially good for men with thinning hair.

What it does: "Master" is light, not too viscous. Unlike other hair grooms that spray on, "Master" does not add a harsh, metallic look. Unlike most competitive liquids, "Master" does not give a slicked-down, greasy look.

For men with thinning hair, "Master" lets a man comb or brush his hair after an all-over spray. It does not plaster the hair down, the strands do not stick together. This makes for a maximum separation of strands and therefore a maximum of hiding of skin. "Master" gently sets and holds hair exactly as it is combed or brushed. It also adds a little lustre but is not blatant or obvious.

The package: Unique in its field, "Master" is packaged in a light metal can (with a plastic cap) in the shape of an Aladdin's lamp. From base to peak: three and one-half inches. From end to end: seven inches. Its color is copper.

Distribution: Nation-wide. Drug stores,˙ department stores, specialty shops, and barber shops. The maker of "Master," the famous Man-Groom Company, has tested barber shop distribution in five cities and has found it an ideal (and little-used) way to distribute this product.

The price: $1.49 a unit.

Ad budget: $2 million annually, most of it in TV spots and news programs.

Assignment

a. Write a 60-second TV commercial (film). Use the _____ structure.

b. Write a 30-second commercial (live). Use the _____ structure.

c. Do a storyboard for each, using tear-out storyboard sheets. Number each panel to correlate with each scene.

d. Do the TV script form for each. Your video directions should be more detailed in this script form. Tear out and hand in, with this assignment page.

NOTE: There are no budget restrictions for the 60-second spot, but the 30-second spot is done at a local TV station using a local announcer.

Assignment notes:

Critique:

Television Storyboard

Student Name: Advertiser:

Date Submitted: Product or Service:

Structure: Commercial Length:

Video:

Audio:

Video:

Audio:

Video:

Audio:

Television Script Sheet

Student Name: Advertiser:

Date Submitted: Product or Service:

Structure: Commercial Length:

VIDEO	AUDIO

"KWIK 'N KOOL"

As an exercise in creativity, here is an opportunity to plan and prepare a commercial without having an actual one of the same type as a guide or idea starter. All of the pertinent details concerning the nature and purpose of, and the market for, the product for which you are to create the commercial are given below. The specific nature of the suggested commercial in this particular case is outlined under "Assignment." The product is a hypothetical one and the name is fictitious. It is called "Kwik 'n Kool" and is a powdered fruit drink.

Background information

Product: "Kwik 'n Kool" is a powdered fruit drink. Its granules dissolve in hot or cold water. It contains an artificial sweetener and imitation fruit flavor. There are five "Kwik 'n Kool" fruit flavors: orange, strawberry, lime, lemon, and "Oahu" (a combination citrus and pineapple).

The taste and flavor closely approximate natural fruit. But "Kwik 'n Kool" has no appreciable health benefit. It is a coolant, a refresher during the summer months, its peak selling season.

One package makes two quarts.

Each flavor can be used alone or in combination with others. All five flavors together might be used as a punch or as the basis for a party punch.

Children can easily mix and make "Kwik 'n Kool."

The market: Wherever there is hot weather, water, and ice cubes. Ninety percent of the consumption of "Kwik 'n Kool" is by children from 5 to 15 years of age. Adult use accounts for 3 percent and the 16 to 21 age bracket consumes 7 percent.

"Kwik 'n Kool" has only 15 percent of the powdered fruit drink market. Its biggest competitor has a 54 percent share.

The package: Each flavor comes packed in a three- by five-inch flat aluminum foil envelope, sealed around all four edges. The name, "Kwik 'n Kool" is in free-hand script diagonally across the face of the front of the package with a picture of its fruit (flavor) and its name across the lower part of the front. Directions for mixing are printed on the back of the package.

Distribution: Supermarkets and specialty food stores, both chains and independents (but it has to fight for shelf space against its big competitor).

The price: Fifteen cents per package (two cents less than its major competition).

Ad budget: One million dollars annually against its competitor's four million.

Assignment

a. Write a 60-second TV commercial (film). Use the _____ structure.

b. Write a 30-second TV commercial (tape). Use the _____ structure.

c. Do a storyboard for each, using tear-out storyboard sheets. Number each panel to correlate with each scene.

d. Do the TV script form for each. Your video directions should be more detailed in this script form. Tear out and hand in, with this assignment page.

NOTE: There are no budget restrictions for the 60-second spot, but the 30-second version is to be planned as a spin-off, utilizing footage shot for the 60.

Assignment notes:

Critique:

Television Storyboard

Student Name: Advertiser:

Date Submitted: Product or Service:

Structure: Commercial Length:

Video:				
Audio:				

Video:				
Audio:				

Video:				
Audio:				

Television Script Sheet

Student Name: Advertiser:

Date Submitted: Product or Service:

Structure: Commercial Length:

VIDEO	AUDIO

"GRO-SLO"

As an exercise in creativity, here is an opportunity to plan and prepare a commercial without having an actual one of the same type as a guide or idea starter. All of the pertinent details concerning the nature and purpose of, and the market for, the product for which you are to create the commercial are given below. The specific nature of the suggested commercial in this particular case is outlined under "Assignment." The product is a hypothetical one and the name is fictitious. It is called "Gro-Slo" and is designed to inhibit the growth of grass.

Background information

Product: "Gro-Slo"—a grass growth inhibitor.

What it is: A chemical compound produced in pellet form. Each pellet is one and one-quarter inches in diameter and has four small holes (arranged like a button). Grass-green in color. Toxic. (Pellets should be kept away from children and pets but will not harm them once applied to grass.) A special applicator need be purchased just once. It attaches to the standard garden hose for application.

What it does: "Gro-Slo" grass growth inhibitor pellets are placed in the special plastic attachment to the hose (between hose and nozzle). As the water is forced through the attachment, it is also forced through and around the pellets. The pellets eventually dissolve, but until they do the water becomes the carrier of the chemical solution and dispenses this solution over the lawn to be treated.

Once the "Gro-Slo" solution is broadcast, the chemical goes to work on leaf and root. It retards the growth of grass—even crab grass.

Even rain will not affect "Gro-Slo" but actually helps it reach the roots. One application covers 1,000 square feet of lawn. Three applications from April through September should suffice.

"Gro-Slo" can be applied early in the spring or immediately after the first cutting of the lawn to the desired height.

The package: The original purchase will be a package 10 by 4 inches in size. It will contain the plastic attachment (with a built-in screen to hold the pellets against the rush of water) and a plastic bag containing a dozen pellets. A printed set of instructions is included. Instructions are also printed on the box.

Subsequent packages of pellets can be bought without the applicator attachment for the hose. These packages are 5 by 1½ by 1½ inches in size.

The distribution: National. Sold in hardware stores, both independents and chains, garden centers, specialty stores, and large discount stores.

The price: Original package: $9.95. Pellet packages: $4.95.

Ad budget: $500,000 annually.

Assignment

a. Write a 60-second introductory commercial (film). Use the _____ structure.

b. Write a 30-second follow-up commercial (live, local). Use the _____ structure.

c. Do a storyboard for each, using tear-out storyboard sheets. Number each panel to correlate with each scene.

d. Do the TV script form for each. Your video directions should be more detailed in this script form. Tear out and hand in with this assignment page.

NOTE: There are no budget restrictions for the 60-second spot. For the 30-second commercial, you will have two cameras and can use props, cards, lighting effects, and slides.

Assignment notes:

Critique:

Television Storyboard

Student Name: Advertiser:

Date Submitted: Product or Service:

Structure: Commercial Length:

Video:

Audio:

Video:

Audio:

Video:

Audio:

Television Script Sheet

Student Name: Advertiser:

Date Submitted: Product or Service:

Structure: Commercial Length:

VIDEO	AUDIO

AAAA American Association of Advertising Agencies, or the 4 A's. A national organization of advertising agencies devoted to standardizing procedures and upgrading the business level of its members.

Above the line Motion picture, television, or radio costs relating to artistic or creative elements in production (writing, acting, directing, music, etc.). (Compare with **Below the line**.)

Abstract set A non-representational setting using elements such as drapes, columns, steps, platforms, free-standing flats with various textures and geometrical forms, etc. Such a setting has no definite locale, but may suggest one.

Academy field When you look through the lens of a motion picture camera, you see two sets of lines framing the rectangular scene. The larger represents what will be seen when the film is projected on a regular screen; this is "academy field" or "academy framing." The smaller set of lines defines the TV field (or "TV cutoff") and shows what will appear on the TV screen. In filming a TV commercial, all essential elements in a scene should be confined to the smaller area.

Academy leader On a TV commercial print, or other film print, there is a section of film with a series of "countdown" numbers to enable the projectionist to cue the opening scene or title of the picture.

Across the board A show which airs at the same time five days a week. So called because it appears straight across the program board each of the first five days.

Action Any movement that takes place in front of a camera or on film. Any movement which carries the story forward and develops the plot.

A.D. Abbreviation for assistant director; a member of the production crew who handles details relating to the actual shooting of a commercial, such as cast and crew calls, adherence to production schedules, etc.

Adjacencies Commercials or programs that immediately precede or follow another.

Ad lib To extemporize lines or music not written into the script or the musical score.

Advertising Council The joint body of the AAAA and the ANA (Association of National Advertisers) and media, through which public service projects are developed and channeled to advertisers for their support (e.g., Smokey the Bear, Cancer Crusade, etc.).

Affiliate A television or radio station associated by contract with a network.

AFTRA Abbreviation for American Federation of Television and Radio Artists, a member of AFL, made up of actors, singers, announcers, etc. It is concerned only with commercials made on video tape or televised live; regulates wage scales for its members. Screen Actors Guild (SAG) serves the same function for talent appearing in filmed commercials. Many performers belong to both unions.

Aided recall A research interviewing technique in which the respondent is given a hint or reminder to elicit a meaningful response. The opposite of this is a "free response" in which the person being interviewed is not given a hint.

Aircheck A recording, either audio, video, or both, of an actual broadcast. It serves as a file copy of a program or commercial for an agency, a sponsor or a competitive sponsor.

Alternate sponsorship When two advertisers share a single program with one advertiser dominant one week, and the other the following week (or whenever the programs are scheduled).

Angle of view Amount of horizontal area of a scene which registers on a lens. Varies in proportion to size of lens, from narrow to wide angle.

Angle shot A camera shot taken from any position except straight on the subject.

Animation Creating an illusion of motion by photographing a series of drawings so that we see drawings that move. Usually done in a cartoon style. Sometimes combined with live action on film.

Announcement spot Brief commercial not integrated into the program.

Announcer 1) The member of a radio or television station staff assigned the duty of introducing and describing program features; 2) the station staff member who delivers a commercial live; 3) the talent who delivers the commercial message (or part of it) either on camera or as a voice-over.

Answer print The first "completed" print of a commercial for client approval. It contains picture, voice track, music, opticals, etc. Color correction and sound levels may be changed before the commercial is telecast.

Arc A strong, blue-white light which glows as a result of electricity sparking across two carbon electrodes (as opposed to a filament which glows from heat).

Arri Nickname for an Arriflex camera, 35mm, widely used in making filmed commercials.

ASCAP American Society of Composers, Authors and Publishers; a music-licensing organization.

Audience accumulation An increase in audience achieved by broadcasting a program in a series rather than just once.

Audience composition A term that refers to a classification of the individuals or the households in a television or radio audience into various categories. Common categories for individuals are age and sex groupings (e.g., men, women, teenagers, and children). Common categories for households are based on the number of members of the household, age or education of the head of the household, household income, and so forth.

Audience flow The statistical composition of the total audience of a program showing the parts 1) retained from the previous program, 2) transferred from another station, and 3) tuned in for the first time.

Audience profile A demographic description of the people exposed to a program or commercial.

Audience share The number or proportion of all home sets in use that are tuned to a particular program.

Audimeter An electronic rating research device. This device is used by the A. C. Nielsen Company to record the radio and TV tuning of sets in selected homes.

Audio The sound portion of a TV broadcast.

Audition A tryout of actors, announcers, musicians, or programs.

Availability In broadcasting, a time period available for purchase by an agency for an advertiser. For talent, the word is used to refer to the artist's lack of conflict either in a product category or for a recording or shooting date.

Average audience rating A type of rating computed for some specified interval of time, such as for the length of a television or radio program or for a 15- or 30-minute period.

Background A broadcasting sound effect, musical or otherwise, used behind or under the dialogue or other program elements. In TV storyboards, the letters "BG" refer to the setting behind the actors, figures, or products in the foreground.

Back light Illumination from behind the subject and opposite the camera.

Back to back A broadcast situation in which two or more commercials directly follow each other without a break. (Also called "piggyback.")

Balop Generally, any opaque projector or the slides and artwork prepared for it. The projector consists of 1) an illuminated stage or surface to hold the object to be televised, and 2) a lens placed to project the image on the tube in the pick-up camera. Multistage balops permit dissolves, superimpositions and simple animation.

Balopticon (balops) A type of television animation made possible through the use of a Balopticon machine, usually in a TV station.

Basic network The section of a national television or radio network covering the more populous markets.

BCU (TCU, ECU) Extremely narrow angle picture. Big close-up. Tight close-up. Extreme close-up.

Below the line Motion picture, television, or radio costs relating to the technical or material elements in production (props, sets, equipment, staging services, etc.)

Billboard Announcement at the beginning of a broadcast which lists the sponsor and/or products featured in the program.

Bit A small part in a television program or commercial.

Bridge Music or sound effect linking two scenes in a TV or radio program.

Business Actor's movement, especially with props; action used to add interest to a program or commercial.

Busy Describes a setting or background that is too elaborate thereby competing with or obscuring the viewer's attention from the actors or object which should predominate.

Buy-out Compensation for a performer not according to the prevailing scale with residual benefits, but in one complete and final sum.

Call letters Initials assigned by the Federal Communications Commission to identify a station.

Camera rehearsal Similar to a dress rehearsal in stage vernacular, where all talent is present and in costume and the complete production is shot by cameramen for final check before telecasting.

Channel A band of radio frequencies assigned to a given radio or TV station, or assigned to other broadcasting purposes.

Circulation The number of households or individuals, regardless of where located, that are estimated to be in the audience of a given television or radio network or station at least once during some specified period of time (e.g., one week or one month). Thus, circulation is simply a term used to describe the size of the cumulative audience of a network or a station over some period of time.

Class (A, B, C) rates The charges or fees for different time segments on a TV or radio station. The most desirable and costly TV time is usually between 6 and 11 p.m. Rates vary from city to city and from station to station.

Clear 1) To obtain legal permission from responsible sources to use a musical selection, photograph, film clip, or quotation for use in an advertisement. 2) To arrange for approval from a station for a certain time slot for a program or commercial.

Close-up A shot of an individual with the camera moved in close so that only the head and shoulders fill the screen. A big close-up (BCU) may include only the head or perhaps just the eyes. A close-up shot (CU) may also be taken of an object.

Closed circuit Television program that is distributed to specific television receivers but not telecast to the public.

Coincidental Method of checking the viewers of a program by phoning a sample of possible viewers while the program is in progress.

Commercial The advertiser's message on television or radio.

Continuity 1) Script for a television or radio program. 2) The flow or sequential development of a commercial.

Control room Room adjacent to the television studio, or recording studio, from which the video and/or audio is coordinated.

Cost per thousand The ratio of the cost of a television or radio advertisement (in dollars) to a number of households (in thousands) or to a number of individuals (in thousands) estimated to be in the audience at the time the advertisement is broadcast. The term is more fully referred to as "cost per thousand households (or homes)" or as "cost per thousand viewers."

Coverage Conceptually, the number of households or individuals, regardless of where located, that are able to receive a given television or radio station or group of stations.

Cowcatcher An isolated commercial announcement at the beginning of a program which advertises a "secondary" product of the sponsor. This secondary product is not mentioned in the program itself.

Crab dolly Generally, a camera move in which the camera pans the subject while the dolly (the camera's moveable base) is being moved.

Crawl Graphics (usually credit copy) that move slowly up the screen; usually mounted on a drum which can also be called a "crawl."

Cross-fade In television, the fading out of one picture and the simultaneous fading in of another. In radio, the fading out of dialogue, sound, or music while simultaneously fading in other dialogue, sound, or music.

CU Close-up shot. Narrow angle picture. Usually bust or head shot of person or full screen image of object.

Cue 1) The final words of an announcer's speech or actor's line used as a signal for another actor or announcer to begin. 2) A sound or musical effect. 3) A manual or audio signal from a director calling for action.

Cut 1) A signal to stop performers. 2) The deletion of program material to fit a prescribed period of time. 3) The most simple transition from one TV commercial scene to another—where the final frame of one scene changes abruptly to that of another scene.

Cut-in The insertion of a local announcement on cue into a network or transcribed program. Also termed a "cut-in announcement" or a "local cut-in."

Cut to 1) A fast switch from the picture on one camera to the picture on another. 2) An abrupt change of scene without a dissolve or wipe.

Demographic characteristics As used in broadcast research, a broad term that refers to the various social and economic characteristics of a group of households, or a group of individuals. For example, the term is used to refer to characteristics such as the number of members of a household, age of head of household, occupation of head of household, education of household members, and annual household income.

Depth of field The distance within which a subject can move toward or away from the camera without going out of focus, assuming no camera adjustment.

Diary method A panel method designed to study broadcast audiences for short periods of time, usually one week.

Diorama Miniature setting, complete in detail and perspective, used as a means of establishing large locations impossible to construct or re-stage in the studio.

Director 1) In TV and radio programming, the person responsible for the rehearsal and performance. 2) For commercials, the person who rehearses actors, announcers, guides cameramen, orders lighting effects, and works with the producer—in short, the person in charge on the set or location.

Dissolve (DS or DISS) 1) A combination fade-in and fade-out; a new scene appears while the preceding scene vanishes. When an object in the first scene apparently remains on screen for the second scene, it is called a "match dissolve." 2) Transitional device to indicate lapse of time by shifting the camera image slowly from one picture to another. 3) The overlapping fade-out of one picture and fade-in of another.

Dolly A moveable carriage usually mounted on four wheels which carries either a camera or a camera and cameraman.

Dolly camera TV camera mounted on small boom which is mounted on four-wheel base. Has advantage of greater height and mobility. It requires a special dolly pusher.

Dolly in To move in from a distance for a close-up by means of a camera mounted on a dolly.

Dolly out Reverse of dolly in. (Dolly back.)

Down and under A direction denoting that voices, music, and sound effects should now be heard at a lower level.

Drop-in In broadcasting, local commercial inserted in a nationally sponsored network program.

Dry runs Those rehearsals previous to camera rehearsals where business, lines, sets, etc., are perfected.

Dubbing 1) Recording actor's and/or announcer's lip sync to film already shot. 2) A copying of an audio tape.

ECU Abbreviation for extreme close-up. A shot showing only a portion of a face or other object. (See also: **BCU, TCU**.)

Establishing shot View of a scene wide and deep enough to establish the relationships of the people and objects in it.

E.T. Electrical transcription. Similar to a record except that it is produced solely for radio and television stations.

Extra A person, usually one of many, used in background shots, crowd shots, parties, etc. Such persons generally have no lines or dialogue.

Fade in To gradually increase the intensity of a video picture from black to full scene.

Fade out From full brightness a picture gradually disappears until the screen is dark. The decreasing of signal strength.

Fixed focus Focus of lens is not changed regardless of what movement takes place in front of the camera.

Flash cut To intersperse scenes of a second or less.

Flat Lack of contrast in screen image. Also, term for a scenic unit.

Floor manager Production man who heads crew in live television studio. Transmits control director's instructions to actors and others on set.

"Follow" shot Camera follows movement of subject without necessarily moving itself.

Frame In motion pictures, a single picture of the many that make up the whole. In television, the field of view in any particular shot. Adjustments in this are known as framing. An improper adjustment is off frame. When the subject crowds the sides of the picture, it is tight framing; when there is plenty of room, it is loose framing.

Free lance A self-employed person who works independently, not employed by an agency or company.

Freeze frame A film technique of holding a particular frame still on screen for a desired length. Often used at the close of a commercial.

Fringe time In television, the hours before or after prime viewing hours.

From the top Order to start rehearsal from the very beginning of the musical number or script. May also refer to the start of a scene currently being rehearsed.

Full shot A full-length view of actors or talent.

Go to black Picture is gradually faded out; same as fade to black, fade out.

Golden time Whenever filming of a TV commercial runs overtime, the costs mount rapidly; this time is considered to be "golden."

Grip The general handyman available on the set for odd jobs such as moving or adjusting sets or repairing props.

Hand-hold To make a shot with the camera held in the hands. Also, a handle which can be mounted on a camera for this purpose.

Head shot A close-up of an actor's or announcer's head, usually from the sholders up.

Hiatus A break in the advertiser's broadcast schedule.

Hitchhike A short commercial tagged on the end of a program, advertising another product of the company sponsoring the program. When at the front, it is a "cowcatcher."

ID Station identification; a 10-second spot on television used at station breaks. Time enough for the product name and claim—and a lot of creative ingenuity.

Integrated commercial A multiple product TV commercial in which two or more products are presented within the framework of a single announcement.

Interlock Any arrangement permitting the synchronous presentation of picture and matching sound from separate films. The simplest consists of a mechanical link connnecting projector and sound reproducer, both being driven by a common synchronous drive.

Key lighting Pin-point, intense light focused on a small area for highlight effect.

Kinescope The tube currently used in receivers or monitors on which the TV picture is reproduced. Trade name developed by RCA.

Kinescope film Television program filmed directly from a kinescope tube.

Kinescope recording A reproduction on film of a TV program or commercial taken directly from the face or screen of the kinescope receiver tube.

Lap dissolve Cross fading of one scene or image over another. Momentarily both pictures are visible. One picture disappears as another picture appears.

Leader (academy leader) The film that precedes the commercial opening. Usually 10 seconds. It has positioning and focus references to guide the video engineer, and numbers sequenced in seconds from nine down to three. Then the film is black for three seconds before the opening frame of the commercial.

"Limbo" shot Pictures taken against non-recognized background. Often used with close-ups where background is non-essential.

Level The amount or quantity of loudness of sound. Also, level of light.

Lip-synchronization (lip-snyc) Recording of a voice or voices to match the exact movement of actors' lips in a film already recorded. Or it can mean the filming of scenes with actors' lips moving to match a pre-recorded track.

Live In television, a program or commercial that is being telecast as it originates.

Location The place or area away from a film studio where a commercial or other part might be filmed.

Logotype (logo) The sponsor's or brand name's identifying signature or trademark.

LS Long shot. A full view of set or background usually including full-length view of actor or actors.

Make-good Credit for a missed commercial or program or re-broadcast in a comparable time period to make up for one unavoidably cancelled, omitted, or not shown clearly or in its entirety.

Matting (matte) A technique in which one part of a picture is photographed in one location and another in a different location and then the two combined in the printing process so that they appear to have been photographed at the same time and place.

Medium shot Obviously, somewhere between a close-up and a long shot.

Mix The sound studio session at which two or three or more sound tracks are combined.

Mobile unit Field equipment housed in special trucks for the televising or taping of an event remote from the studio.

Monitor A control kinescope used by personnel (producer, switcher, technical director) to check and preview camera pick-ups or on-the-air pictures.

Montage A sequence of short scenes which together convey an idea that could not be conveyed by any one of them alone. Sometimes several of the scenes appear on the screen at once; sometimes one blends into another; sometimes they appear in quick succession.

Move in A storyboard designation describing camera movement toward the subject being photographed. Also "zoom in."

Moviola Special machine (with sound equipment) used mainly by editors for viewing film in small size.

MS Abbreviation for medium shot. Somewhere between a close-up (CU) and a long shot (LS).

MS and MCU Medium shot and medium close-up. Camera instructions indicating subject should be seen in relation to some but not all other elements in scene, the latter being more restrictive than the former.

Narrator An off-camera or background voice. Refers also to on-camera spokesman relating story line of script.

Network Interconnecting broadcasting stations for the simultaneous broadcasting of TV or radio programs.

NTI Nielsen Television Index. A limited but projectable rating system that helps determine a TV program's viewing audience.

Off-camera An actor or announcer's voice which is heard although the actor or announcer does not appear on screen.

Off-screen narration Any narration that is not lip sync. Also referred to as "voice-over."

On-camera 1) Actor or announcer delivers his lines as he appears on the screen. 2) Whatever is included within the scope of the lens.

Opaques Non-transparent artwork or visuals (i.e., a photo, postcard, picture from magazine, etc.). Variations: 1) "Flip": opaque artwork or titles mounted on heavy card, flipped vertically or horizontally. 2) Draw cards: some material pulled manually or mechanically from its position, either horizontally, vertically, or obliquely.

Open end 1) A broadcast in which the commercial spots are added locally. 2) A network commercial complete except for final seconds of audio or video which are cut in locally.

Optical Special photographic effects, such as the dissolving of one scene into another, wiping out of one scene and appearance of another (wipe), a motion picture within the film (matte shot), grouping of several scenes simultaneously (montage), etc.

Optical view finder Device on a camera used by the cameraman to accurately frame and focus the scene to be televised or filmed.

Over scale A rate of pay that is more than the standard rate of pay for a particular job. Star personalities often demand, and receive, over-scale compensation.

Over-the-shoulder shot A camera shot of a performer from across the shoulder of the character to whom he is speaking.

Pan An abbreviation of panoramic. To "pan" is to move the camera, either left or right, without moving the dolly or base. A movement up or down is properly called a "tilt," but on some scripts you will see the direction "pan up" instead of "tilt up."

Participating program A TV or radio show in which a number of advertisers have their products featured or mentioned.

Pedestal camera TV camera mounted on pneumatically controlled base allowing for greater movement in studio. Must be moved by cameraman or operator.

Picture resolution The clarity with which the TV image appears on the TV screen.

Piggyback A one-minute time segment in which a sponsor can show two commercials, each featuring a different product.

Playback The replaying of a tape for review and correction purposes.

Positive A projection print from negative film. The true picture.

Pre-empt Telecasting time made available for a special event, which takes the place of the regularly scheduled program.

Prime time A continuous period of not less than three hours of the broadcast day during which the station's audience is the greatest. In television, usually from 7 to 11 p.m. in the East and from 6 to 10 p.m. in the Midwest and West.

Prism lens A special lens with several facets that breaks one picture up into many. Used for special effects—as when multiple images of a dancer are seen on many parts of the screen.

Process shot A shot involving an unusual process of some sort, especially rear projection (either still or in motion), with live action taking place in front of the projected picture; shooting through glass on which scenes are painted, with live action taking place behind it; or the use of miniature sets combined with live action in such a way as to create the impression of reality.

Producer The coordinator and overseer of all aspects of getting a TV storyboard onto film or tape. Responsible for budget, schedules, talent, and for meeting deadlines.

Product protection In television, the assurance to an advertiser of a time lapse between his commercial and that of a competitor. Given by a station or network, such protection assurance is usually up to 15 minutes.

Promo Spot ad plugging a program, station, or service.

Props From "properties." All the articles in a production that are the property of the producing company or are rented by the company; notably furnishings and decorations, but including an infinite variety of items, large and small, from ashtrays to zipguns.

Pull-back A storyboard designation describing camera movement away from the subject being photographed. (Also zoom-back, move-back.)

Rate card Chart which lists the cost of broadcast time on a station based on the length of the announcement and the number of times used on the air.

Rating The percentage of a statistical sample of families who have a radio and/or television set available who reported hearing or viewing a particular program when interviewed.

Rating points In broadcast, the percent of potential audience tuned to a specific station for a specific program.

Rear projection A device which allows actors to be filmed in front of a screen on which is projected—from behind—a special background. A substitute for expensive location shooting. A device that allows an actor or announcer to be on camera while the background can be anything you want.

Release print Final print of commercial film or kinescope to be delivered to TV station, client, or agency.

Remote Telecast originated outside the studio.

Reportage The style of shooting film with a hand-held camera, available light, and candidness. Kind of a cinema verite' technique that gives the film added realism, an unrehearsed quality.

Run-through Rehearsal.

SAG Screen Actors Guild. The union of performers in films who work for established scales of pay. The only time you may use a player who is not a member of SAG is when you are showing actual jobs or activities that non-SAG people alone are qualified to do.

Saturation A media term denoting high frequency of advertising impressions during a concentrated period of time.

Scale The standard, established rates of pay for members of film and television unions.

Scene A completed piece of action or dialogue. Usually all the action and dialogue taking place continuously with the same background. Also, a setting or location for action.

Segue In music, the bridge or transposition from one theme to another.

Set A TV scene used or constructed in the studio where action takes place and is filmed.

Share of audience Generally, the percentage of the aggregate television or radio audience in some specified area at some specified time that is in the broadcast area of a given network, station, or program. Frequently referred to simply as "share."

Shock cut Sudden, abrupt cut to a particular dramatic scene or action.

Shooting date The day designated for the start of actual filming.

Signature The name and/or logo or trademark of the advertiser.

Simulcast The simultaneous playing of a program over television and radio. (Also, a stereo broadcast over two radio stations.)

Slide A title or picture on a single frame of 35mm film that is projected into the camera. Called "transparencies," they are invariably glass mounted. (May be other than 35mm in size.)

Sneak To bring in a sound or a music cue at low volume without distracting the attention of the listener. After an effect has served its purpose, it may be "sneaked out" in like manner.

SOF Sound on film.

Sound effects (SFX) Various devices or recordings used to simulate lifelike sounds. On storyboards, use the abbreviation SFX before you indicate the sound effect you wish.

Spec sheet A list of specifications about a product or advertiser, to be included in a commercial by an announcer who creates his own wording for the commercial. (Also, fact sheet.)

Special effects Miniatures, diorama, or various electrical, film, or mechanical devices used to simulate impressive backgrounds, massive titles, etc. Any trick device used to achieve scenic or dramatic effects impossible of actual or full-scale production in the TV studio.

Splice To join together two pieces of film with film cement.

Split screen A special effect utilizing two or more cameras so that two or more scenes are visible simultaneously on separate parts of the screen (e.g., two people holding a telephone conversation).

Sponsor The firm or individual that pays for broadcast time and talent.

Spot 1) Spotlight. 2) Time segment of one minute or less sold by stations for advertisements.

Spot commercial Commercial of one minute or less, usually on film or tape. It may be shown within a program or adjacent to it.

Spot television Generally, commercial messages within shows not totally sponsored by one firm, or commercials shown during station breaks, as opposed to commercials within the framework of one sponsor's program. Also, the spotting of commercials in selected geographical locations.

Sound track The recorded audio portion of a filmed or taped commercial.

Station break Brief break in the programming so station may identify itself. An "hour" network program actually runs only 59 minutes and 25 seconds, the next five seconds being used for network identification, the following 20 for a commercial, and the final 10 for another commercial including two seconds for local station identification. A half-hour network program runs 29 minutes and 25 seconds.

Still A still photograph or other illustrative material that may be used in a TV broadcast.

Stock shot A scene not filmed especially for the production but taken from film files or a film library.

Stop motion Film taken by exposing one frame instead of many frames at a time. Object or objects are usually moved a fraction of an inch for each exposure according to a predetermined pattern.

Storyboard Drawings or photographs arranged in sequence that show the visual continuity of a commercial, with copy adjacent to each picture describing the video action and the audio portion.

Studio 1) At a TV station, room from which programs emanate. 2) At a film production house, the room in which commercials are filmed.

Super Abbreviation for superimposition. One picture (usually opaque titles) is imposed in front of another picture, and both are seen simultaneously.

Sync Synchronization; the simultaneous projection of picture and sound; also the electronic pulses of picture transmitter and receiver must be synchronized to produce a stable image on the television screen.

Tag An addition to a commercial, announcement, or musical gimmick which acts as a finale to that segment.

TCU Tight close-up; narrow angle picture. (See also, **BCU, ECU**.)

Take 1) Switching directly from one picture camera to another picture or camera, as "take one, take two." 2) Individual filmed or taped sequences or scenes.

Talent An all-inclusive word referring to actors, announcers, musicians, or performers.

Technical director The director of all camera or video facilities from a television station.

Telephoto lens A very narrow angle lens which produces large images at extreme distance; frequently used at sporting events, etc.

Teleprompter Patented machine on which a large version of the script can be unrolled at any desired speed, operated out of camera range to prompt actors; usually mounted on camera near lens turret. Reader appears to look almost directly at the viewer when using Teleprompter on live camera.

Televise To transmit a picture electronically using TV equipment.

Telop Opaque photograph or drawing projected by the telop projector.

Tight shot A picture that fills the screen with a single object of interest so that no background detail distracts from it.

Tilt Camera movement, pivoting on horizontal axis, up or down.

Tilt-up A storyboard designation describing an upward pan of the camera. (Tilt-down, obviously, is the reverse movement.)

Title crawl Device for moving a series of titles across the screen, appearing at the bottom, disappearing at the top. Often a motor-driven drum.

Title drum Large drum on which title sheets can be fastened for credit supers; same as crawl.

Titles Any title used on a TV program or commercial. Can be motion picture film, card, slides, etc.

Transparency A technique whereby illustrative or written material is placed on a transparent surface through which background material may be seen as the transparency is picked up by the TV camera.

Treatment An intermediate step between synopsis and script where the complete TV story, commercial, or production is completed.

Truck Movement of studio camera, left or right, parallel to plane of action.

Trucking The camera moving beside a character or object which is in motion.

Truck shot A camera, mounted on a moveable dolly, is guided along a certain prescribed path marked on the studio floor. This gives an effect of moving toward, past, or away from whatever is to be filmed.

TVB Television Bureau of Advertising.

Two shot Often printed "2-shot"; refers to a picture in which two persons are seen. ("3-shot" includes three people.)

Viewfinder Small television set on top of the camera in which the cameraman sees the picture he is photographing.

Viewing lens The lens on a TV camera used by the cameraman to view the field of action.

Video The visual, pictorial portion of a television program, announcement, or commercial.

Videotape recording An electronic system which permits recording of video and audio on a continuous strip of tape. It requires no laboratory processing, can be rewound and played back immediately, and can be edited immediately after recording. Film is often transferred to video tape for use in telecasting.

Voice-over (VO) In television, a commercial, film, or live sequence where an actor's or annoucer's voice is heard, but the person is not seen.

Whip shot A fast pan shot, blurring the action on the screen.

Whiz pan Camera swung very rapidly left to right or right to left, blurring the scene. Used as dramatic device to shift from one scene to another or one object of interest to another, or for comic effects, simulating doubletake. Also known as blur pan, swish pan, whip shot, etc.

Wide-angle lens A special lens that permits a greater view of the field, left and right.

Wide-angle shot A shot that makes it possible for the camera to cut a wide scene from a shallow depth.

Wide shot A shot which covers a large area.

Wipe Optical effect in which a line or object appears to move across the screen revealing a new picture. A wipe may stop midway and become a split-screen effect.

Wipe over Optical film or printing effect by which one scene or image moves into another geometrically.

XCU Extreme close-up; same as ECU.

Zoom The change in focal length of a special lens (Zoomar lens) which gives the effect of moving either toward or away from an object.

Zoomar Adjustable lens which can zoom from a focal length of one size to another without loss of focus or light.

Zoom lens A special lens on motion picture and TV camera which permits slow or rapid movement either toward or away from the photographed subject. Can be used in studios or on location. Can be used to cover a great distance quickly.

Section IV
Advertising Standards

Early in this century, business people influenced by the philosophy of *caveat emptor* (let the buyer beware) began to contend with others having a growing sense of honesty and responsibility in the way advertising was used. While a majority of products were promoted with fairness, there were dramatic examples of outrageous claims of performance and benefit, notably patent medicines and health products. Public pressure groups and Congress acted. Regulatory laws went into effect. Industry and media developed codes of self-regulation.

Today, the consumer continues to be protected and every copywriter must be aware of consumer interest group pressures, local and federal statutes and regulations, and advertising industry guidelines as well as media regulations.

In terms of specific advertising practices, the law looks closely at what the seller offers the buyer in regard to truth, fairness, and honesty. As ideals, these terms are open to some interpretation.

The interpretation is made by various government agencies such as the Federal Trade Commission which was formed in 1914. The job of the FTC is to protect the public from false advertising and scurrilous business methods, and to preserve free and fair competition in the marketplace. It has responsibility for policing a wider area of the American economy than any other government agency. Not only can it halt what it considers to be dishonest advertising with a "cease and desist" order, the FTC can also proceed against practices that threaten fair competition.

Since the inception of the FTC, the number of regulatory federal agencies has continued to proliferate. More than 20 such bodies exist today, including the Alcohol Tax Unit, the Interstate Commerce Commission, the Federal Power Commission, the National Bureau of Standards, the Food and Drug Administration, the U.S. Postal Service, Securities and Exchange Commission, and, of course, the Federal Communications Commission. The FCC exercises specific controls over broadcast program content and can influence radio and TV stations regarding advertising. Additionally, all states and many local governments have special advertising statutes.

There are laws to protect copyrights, to protect identifying product names, packages, and symbols, to protect an individual's "right of privacy" (written permission to use a person's name or endorsement must be obtained), and to protect a person's reputation against libel or defamation.

Both local and national advertisers have Fair Practice Codes and both work with organized Better Business Bureaus to handle consumer complaints and competitive questions. Advertising agencies as members of the American Association of Advertising Agencies endorse "The Advertising Code of American Businesses" which includes strong statements on truth, honesty, obscenity and bad taste, accuracy, and responsibility.

A significant corollary to government laws and industry codes is self-regulation by the media. This covers not only legal proprieties but also a sense of responsibility to the consuming public in areas of ethics and taste not covered by law. The Code Authority of the National Association of Broadcasters, which follows, illustrates the continuing concern of radio and television stations for self-regulation.

Chapter 19

Radio Advertising Standards

Advertising is the principal source of revenue in the free, competitive American system of broadcasting. It makes possible the presentation to all American people of the finest programs of entertainment, education, and information.

Since the great strength of American radio broadcasting derives from the public respect for and the public approval of its programs, it must be the purpose of each broadcaster to establish and maintain high standards of performance, not only in the selection and production of all programs, but also in the presentation of advertising.

This Code establishes basic standards for all radio broadcasting. The principles of acceptability and good taste within the program standards section govern the presentation of advertising where applicable. In addition, the Code establishes in this section special standards which apply to radio advertising.

General Advertising Standards

1. A commercial radio broadcaster makes his facilities available for the advertising of products and services and accepts commercial presentations for such advertising. However, he shall, in recognition of his responsibility to the public, refuse the facilities of his station to an advertiser where he has good reason to doubt the integrity of the advertiser, the truth of the advertising representation, or the compliance of the advertiser with the spirit and purpose of all applicable legal requirements.

2. In consideration of the customs and attitudes of the communities served, each radio broadcaster should refuse his facilities to the advertisement of products and services, or the use of advertising scripts, which the station has good reason to believe would be objectionable to a substantial and responsible segment of the community. These standards should be applied with judgment and flexibility, taking into consideration the characteristics of the medium, its home and family audience, and the form and content of the particular presentation.

Presentation of Advertising

1. The advancing techniques of the broadcast art have shown that the quality and proper integration of advertising copy are just as important as measurement in time. The measure of a station's service to its audience is determined by its overall performance.

2. The final measurement of any commercial broadcast service is quality. To this, every broadcaster shall dedicate his best efforts.

3. Great care shall be exercised by the broadcaster to prevent the presentation of false, misleading or deceptive advertising. While it is entirely appropriate to present a product in a favorable light and atmosphere, the presentation must not, by copy or demonstration, involve a material deception as to the characteristics or performance of a product.

4. The broadcaster and the advertiser should exercise special caution with the content and presentation of commercials placed in or near programs designed for children. Exploitation of children should be avoided. Commercials directed to children should in no way mislead as to the product's performance and usefulness. Appeals involving matters of health which should be determined by physicians should be avoided.

5. Reference to the results of research, surveys, or tests relating to the product to be advertised shall not be presented in a manner so as to create an impression of fact beyond that established by the study. Surveys, tests, or other research results upon which claims are based must be conducted under recognized research techniques and standards.

Acceptability of Advertisers and Products

In general, because radio broadcasting is designed for the home and the entire family, the following principles shall govern the business classifications:

1. The advertising of hard liquor shall not be accepted.

2. The advertising of beer and wines is accepta-

ble when presented in the best of good taste and discretion.

3. The advertising of spiritualism, occultism, astrology, phrenology, palm-reading, numerology, mind-reading, character-reading, or subjects of a like nature, is not acceptable.

4. Because the advertising of all products and services of a personal nature raises special problems, such advertising, when accepted, should be treated with emphasis on ethics and the canons of good taste, and be presented in a restrained and inoffensive manner.

5. The advertising of lotteries is unacceptable. The advertising of tip sheets and other publications seeking to advertise for the purpose of giving odds or promoting betting is unacceptable.

The advertising of organizations, private or governmental, which conduct legalized betting on sporting contests is acceptable, provided it is limited to institutional type advertising which does not exhort the public to bet.

6. An advertiser who markets more than one product shall not be permitted to use advertising copy devoted to an acceptable product for purposes of publicizing the brand name or other identification of a product which is not acceptable.

7. Care should be taken to avoid presentation of "bait-and-switch" advertising whereby goods or services which the advertiser has no intention of selling are offered merely to lure the customer into purchasing higher-priced substitutes.

8. Advertising should offer a product or service on its positive merits and should refrain from discrediting, disparaging, or unfairly attacking competitors, competing products, other industries, professions, or institutions.

Any identification or comparison of a competitive product or service, by name or other means, should be confined to specific facts rather than generalized statements or conclusions, unless such statements or conclusions are not derogatory in nature.

9. Advertising testimonials should be genuine, and reflect an honest appraisal of personal experience.

10. Advertising by institutions or enterprises offering instruction with exaggerated claims for opportunities awaiting those who enroll, is unacceptable.

11. The advertising of firearms/ammunition is acceptable provided it promotes the product only as sporting equipment and conforms to recognized standards of safety as well as all applicable laws and regulations. Advertisements of firearms/ammunition by mail order is unacceptable.

Advertising of Medical Products

Because advertising of over-the-counter products involving health considerations is of intimate and far-reaching importance to the consumer, the following principles should apply to such advertising:

1. When dramatized advertising material involves statements by doctors, dentists, nurses, or other professional people, the material should be presented by members of such profession reciting actual experience, or it should be made apparent from the presentation itself that the portrayal is dramatized.

2. Because of the personal nature of the advertising of medical products, the indiscriminate use of such words as "Safe," "Without Risk," "Harmless," or other terms of similar meaning, either direct or implied, should not be expressed in the advertising of medical products.

3. Advertising material which offensively describes or dramatizes distress or morbid situations involving ailments is not acceptable.

Time Standards for Advertising Copy

1. The amount of time to be used for advertising should not exceed 18 minutes within any clock hour. The Code Authority, however, for good cause may approve advertising exceeding the above standard for special circumstances.

2. Any reference to another's products or services under any trade name, or language sufficiently descriptive to identify it, shall, except for normal guest identification, be considered as advertising copy.

3. For the purpose of determining advertising limitations, such program types as "classified," "swap shop," "shopping guides," and "farm auction" programs, etc., shall be regarded as containing one and one-half minutes of advertising for each five-minute segment.

Contests

1. Contests shall be conducted with fairness to all entrants, and shall comply with all pertinent laws and regulations.

2. All contest details, including rules, eligibility requirements, opening and termination dates, should be clearly and completely announced or easily accessible to the listening public, and the winners' names should be released as soon as possible after the close of the contest.

3. When advertising is accepted which requests contestants to submit items of product identification or other evidence of purchase of products, reasonable facsimiles thereof should be made acceptable. However, when the award is based upon skill and not upon chance, evidence of purchase may be required.

4. All copy pertaining to any contest (except that

which is required by law) associated with the exploitation or sale of the sponsor's product or service, and all reference to prizes or gifts offered in such connection should be considered a part of and included in the total time limitations heretofore provided (see "Time Standards for Advertising Copy.").

Premiums and Offers

1. The broadcaster should require that full details of proposed offers be submitted for investigation and approval before the first announcement of the offer is made to the public.

2. A final date for the termination of the offer should be announced as far in advance as possible.

3. If a consideration is required, the advertiser should agree to honor complaints indicating dissatisfaction with the premium by returning the consideration.

4. There should be no misleading descriptions or comparisons of any premiums or gifts which will distort or enlarge their value in the minds of the listeners.

Chapter 20
Television Advertising Standards

General Advertising Standards

1. This Code establishes basic standards for all television broadcasting. The principles of acceptability and good taste within the Program Standards Section govern the presentation of advertising where applicable. In addition, the Code establishes in this section special standards which apply to television advertising.

2. A commercial television broadcaster makes his facilities available for the advertising of products and services and accepts commercial presentations for such advertising. However, a television broadcaster should, in recognition of his responsibility to the public, refuse the facilities of his station to an advertiser where he has good reason to doubt the integrity of the advertiser, the truth of the advertising representations, or the compliance of the advertisers with the spirit and purpose of all applicable legal requirements.

3. Identification of sponsorship must be made in all sponsored programs in accordance with the requirements of the Communications Act of 1934, as amended, and the Rules and Regulations of the Federal Communications Commission.

4. Representations which disregard normal safety precautions shall be avoided.

Children shall not be represented, except under proper adult supervision, as being in contact with or demonstrating a product recognized as potentially dangerous to them.

5. In consideration of the customs and attitudes of the communities served, each television broadcaster should refuse his facilities to the advertisement of products and services, or the use of advertising scripts, which the station has good reason to believe would be objectionable to a substantial and responsible segment of the community. These standards should be applied with judgment and flexibility, taking into consideration the characteristics of the medium, its home and family audience, and the form and content of the particular presentation.

6. The advertising of hard liquor (distilled spirits) is not acceptable.

7. The advertising of beer and wines is acceptable only when presented in the best of good taste and discretion, and is acceptable only subject to Federal and local laws. (See Television Code Interpretation No. 4.)

8. Advertising by institutions or enterprises which in their offers of instruction imply promises of employment or make exaggerated claims for the opportunities awaiting those who enroll for courses is generally unacceptable.

9. The advertising of firearms/ammunition is acceptable provided it promotes the product only as sporting equipment and conforms to recognized standards of safety as well as all applicable laws and regulations. Advertisements of firearms/ammunition by mail order are unacceptable. The advertising of fireworks is acceptable subject to all applicable laws.

10. The advertising of fortune-telling, occultism, astrology, phrenology, palm-reading, numerology, mind-reading, character-reading, or subjects of like nature is not permitted.

11. Because all products of a personal nature create special problems, acceptability of such products should be determined with especial emphasis on ethics and the canons of good taste. Such advertising of personal products as is accepted must be presented in a restrained and obviously inoffensive manner.

12. The advertising of tip sheets and other publications seeking to advertise for the purpose of giving odds or promoting betting is unacceptable.

The lawful advertising of governmental organizations which conduct legalized lotteries is acceptable provided such advertising does not unduly exhort the public to bet.

The advertising of private or governmental organizations which conduct legalized betting on sporting contests is acceptable provided such advertising is limited to institutional type announcements which do not exhort the public to bet.

13. An advertiser who markets more than one product should not be permitted to use advertising copy devoted to an acceptable product for purposes of publicizing the brand name or other identification of a product which is not acceptable.

14. "Bait-switch" advertising, whereby goods or services which the advertiser had no intention of selling are offered merely to lure the customer into purchasing higher-priced substitutes, is not acceptable.

15. Personal endorsements (testimonials) shall be genuine and reflect personal experience. They shall contain no statement that cannot be supported if presented in the advertiser's own words.

Presentation of Advertising

1. Advertising messages should be presented with courtesy and good taste; disturbing or annoying material should be avoided; every effort should be made to keep the advertising message in harmony with the content and general tone of the program in which it appears.

2. The role and capability of television to market sponsors' products are well recognized. In turn, this fact dictates that great care be exercised by the broadcaster to prevent the presentation of false, misleading, or deceptive advertising. While it is entirely appropriate to present a product in a favorable light and atmosphere, the presentation must not, by copy or demonstration, involve a material deception as to the characteristics, performance, or appearance of the product.

Broadcast advertisers are responsible for making available, at the request of the Code Authority, documentation adequate to support the validity and truthfulness of claims, demonstrations, and testimonials contained in their commercial messages.

3. The broadcaster and the advertiser should exercise special caution with the content and presentation of television commercials placed in or near programs designed for children. Exploitation of children should be avoided. Commercials directed to children should in no way mislead as to the product's performance and usefulness.

Commercials, whether live, film or tape, within programs initially designed primarily for children under 12 years of age shall be clearly separated from program material by an appropriate device.

Trade name identification or other merchandising practices involving the gratuitous naming of products is discouraged in programs designed primarily for children.

Appeals involving matters of health which should be determined by physicians should not be directed primarily to children.

4. No children's program personality or cartoon character shall be utilized to deliver commercial messages within or adjacent to the programs in which such a personality or cartoon character regularly appears. This provision shall also apply to lead-ins to commercials when such lead-ins contain sell copy or imply endorsement of the product by program personalities or cartoon characters. (Effective September 1975)

5. Appeals to help fictitious characters in television programs by purchasing the advertiser's product or service or sending for a premium should not be permitted, and such fictitious characters should not be introduced into the advertising message for such purposes.

6. Commercials for services or over-the-counter products involving health considerations are of intimate and far-reaching importance to the consumer. The following principles should apply to such advertising:

a. Physicians, dentists, or nurses or actors representing physicians, dentists, or nurses, shall not be employed directly or by implication.
   These restrictions also apply to persons professionally engaged in medical services (e.g., physical therapists, pharmacists, dental assistants, nurses' aides).

b. Visual representations of laboratory settings may be employed, provided they bear a direct relationship to bona fide research which has been conducted for the product or service. (See paragraph 11 under "General Advertising Standards.") In such cases, laboratory-technicians shall be identified as such and shall not be employed as spokesmen or in any other way speak on behalf of the product.

c. Institutional announcements not intended to sell a specific product or service to the consumer and public service announcements by non-profit organizations may be presented by accredited physicians, dentists, or nurses, subject to approval by the broadcaster. An accredited professional is one who has met required qualifications and has been licensed in his resident state.

7. Advertising should offer a product or service on its positive merits and should refrain from discrediting, disparaging, or unfairly attacking competitors, competing products, other industries, professions, or institutions.

8. A sponsor's advertising messages should be confined within the framework of the sponsor's program structure. A television broadcaster should avoid the use of commercial announcements which are divorced from the program either by preceding

the introduction of the program (as in the case of so-called "cowcatcher" announcements) or by following the apparent sign-off of the program (as in the case of so-called trailer or "hitchhike" announcements). To this end, the program itself should be announced and clearly identified, both audio and video, before the sponsor's advertising material is first used, and should be signed off, both audio and video, after the sponsor's advertising material is last used.

9. Since advertising by television is a dynamic technique, a television broadcaster should keep under surveillance new advertising devices so that the spirit and purpose of these standards are fulfilled.

10. A charge for television time to churches and religious bodies is not recommended.

11. Reference to the results of bona fide research, surveys, or tests relating to the product to be advertised shall not be presented in a manner so as to create an impression of fact beyond that established by the work that has been conducted.

Advertising of Medical Products

1. The advertising of medical products presents considerations of intimate and far-reaching importance to the consumer because of the direct bearing on his health.

2. Because of the personal nature of the advertising of medical products, claims that a product will effect a cure and the indiscriminate use of such words as "safe," "without risk," "harmless," or terms of similar meaning should not be accepted in the advertising of medical products on television stations.

3. A television broadcaster should not accept advertising material which in his opinion offensively describes or dramatizes distress or morbid situations involving ailments, by spoken word, sound, or visual effects.

Contests

1. Contests shall be conducted with fairness to all entrants, and shall comply with all pertinent laws and regulations. Care should be taken to avoid the concurrent use of the three elements which together constitute a lottery—prize, chance, and consideration.

2. All contest details, including rules, eligibility requirements, opening and termination dates should be clearly and completely announced and/or shown, or easily accessible to the viewing public, and the winners' names should be released and prizes awarded as soon as possible after the close of the contest.

3. When advertising is accepted which requires contestants to submit items of product identification or other evidence of purchase of products, reasonable facsimiles thereof should be made acceptable

unless the award is based upon skill and not upon chance.

4. All copy pertaining to any contest (except that which is required by law) associated with the exploitation or sale of the sponsor's product or service, and all references to prices or gifts offered in such connection should be considered a part of and included in the total time allowances as herein provided. (See section on "Time Standards for Nonprogram Material.")

Premiums and Offers

1. Full details of proposed offers should be required by the television broadcaster for investigation and approved before the first announcement of the offer is made to the public.

2. A final date for the termination of an offer should be announced as far in advance as possible.

3. Before accepting for telecast offers involving a monetary consideration, a television broadcaster should satisfy himself as to the integrity of the advertiser and the advertiser's willingness to honor complaints indicating dissatisfaction with the premium by returning the monetary considerations.

4. There should be no misleading descriptions or visual representations of any premiums or gifts which would distort or enlarge their value in the minds of the viewers.

5. Assurances should be obtained from the advertiser that premiums offered are not harmful to person or property.

6. Premiums should not be approved which appeal to superstition on the basis of "luck-bearing" powers or otherwise.

Time Standards for Nonprogram Material

In order that the time for nonprogram material and its placement shall best serve the viewer, the following standards are set forth in accordance with sound television practice:

1. Nonprogram material definition: Nonprogram material, in both prime time and all other time, includes billboards, commercials, promotional announcements and all credits in excess of 30 seconds per program, except in feature films. In no event should credits exceed 40 seconds per program. The 40-second limitation on credits shall not apply, however, in any situation governed by a contract entered into before October 1, 1971. Public service announcements and promotional announcements for the same program are excluded from this definition.

2. Allowable time for nonprogram material:
a. In prime time on network affiliated stations, nonprogram material shall not exceed nine minutes 30 seconds in any 60-minute period.

In the event that news programing is included within the three and one-half hour prime-time period, not more than one 30-minute segment of news programing may be governed by time standards applicable to all other time.

Prime time is a continuous period of not less than three and one-half consecutive hours per broadcast day as designated by the station between the hours of 6 p.m. and Midnight.

b. In all other time, nonprogram material shall not exceed 16 minutes in any 60-minute period.

c. Children's programing time: defined as those hours other than prime time in which programs initially designed primarily for children under 12 years of age are scheduled.

Within this time period on Saturday and Sunday, nonprogram material shall not exceed 10 minutes in any 60-minute period after December 31, 1974, and nine minutes 30 seconds in any 60-minute period after December 31, 1975.

Within this time period on Monday through Friday, nonprogram material shall not exceed 14 minutes in any 60-minute period after December 31, 1974, and 12 minutes in any 60-minute period after December 31, 1975.

3. Program interruptions:

a. Definition: A program interruption is any occurrence of nonprogram material within the main body of the program.

b. In prime time, the number of program interruptions shall not exceed two within any 30-minute program, or four within any 60-minute program.

Programs longer than 60 minutes shall be prorated at two interruptions per half-hour.

The number of interruptions in a 60-minute variety show shall not exceed five.

c. In all other time, the number of interruptions shall not exceed four within any 30-minute program period.

d. In children's weekend programing time, as above defined in 2c, the number of program interruptions shall not exceed two within any 30-minute program or four within any 60-minute program.

e. In both prime time and all other time, the following interruption standard shall apply within programs of 15 minutes or less in length: 5-minute program—1 interruption; 10-minute program—2 interruptions; 15-minute program—2 interruptions.

f. News, weather, sports and special events programs are exempt from the interruption standard because of the nature of such programs.

4. No more than four nonprogram material announcements shall be scheduled consecutively within programs, and no more than three nonprogram material announcements shall be scheduled consecutively during station breaks. The consecutive nonprogram material limitation shall not apply to a single sponsor who wishes to further reduce the number of interruptions in the program.

5. A multiple product announcement is one in which two or more products or services are presented within the framework of a single announcement. A multiple product announcement shall not be scheduled in a unit of time less than 60 seconds, except where integrated so as to appear to the viewer as a single message. A multiple product announcement shall be considered integrated and counted as a single announcement if:

a. the products or services are related and interwoven within the framework of the announcement (related products or services shall be defined as those having a common character, purpose, and use); and

b. the voice(s), setting, background, and continuity are used consistently throughout so as to appear to the viewer as a single message.

Multiple product announcements of 60 seconds in length or longer not meeting this definition of integration shall be counted as two or more announcements under this section of the Code. This provision shall not apply to retail or service establishments.

6. The use of billboards, in prime time and all other time, shall be confined to programs sponsored by a single or alternate week advertiser and shall be limited to the products advertised in the program.

7. Reasonable and limited identification of prizes and donors' names where the presentation of contest awards or prizes is a necessary part of program content shall not be included as nonprogram material as defined above.

8. Programs presenting women's service features, shopping guides, fashion shows, demonstrations, and similar material provide a special service to the public in which certain material normally classified as nonprogram is an informative and necessary part of the program content. Because of this, the time standards may be waived by the Code Authority to a reasonable extent on a case-by-case basis.

9. Gratuitous references in a program to a nonsponsor's product or service should be avoided except for normal guest identification.

10. Stationary backdrops or properties in television presentations showing the sponsor's name or product, the name of his product, his trademark or slogan should be used only incidentally and should not obtrude on program interest or entertainment.

Time Standards for Independent Stations

1. Nonprogram elements shall be considered as all-inclusive, with the exception of required credits, legally required station identifications, and "bumpers." Promotion spots and public service announcements, as well as commercials, are to be considered nonprogram elements.

2. The allowed time for nonprogram elements, as defined above, shall not exceed seven minutes in a 30-minute period or multiples thereof in prime time (prime time is defined as any three contiguous hours between 6 p.m. and Midnight, local time), or eight minutes in a 30-minute period or multiples thereof during all other times.

3. Where a station does not carry a commercial in a station break between programs, the number of program interruptions shall not exceed four within any 30-minute program, or seven within any 60-minute program, or 10 within any 90-minute program, or 13 in any 120-minute program. Stations which do carry commercials in station breaks between programs shall limit the number of program interruptions to three within any 30-minute program, or six within any 60-minute program, or nine within any 90-minute program, or 12 in any 120-minute program. News, weather, sports, and special events are exempted because of format.

4. Not more than four nonprogram material announcements as defined above shall be scheduled consecutively. An exception may be made only in the case of a program 60 minutes or more in length, when no more than seven nonprogram elements may be scheduled consecutively by stations who wish to reduce the number of program interruptions.

5. The conditions of paragraphs three and four shall not apply to live sports programs where the program format dictates and limits the number of program interruptions.

Bibliography

Abrahams, Howard P. *Making TV Pay Off*. New York: Fairchild Publications, 1975.

Backman, Jules. *Advertising and Competition*. New York: New York University Press, 1967.

Bellaire, Arthur. *The TV Commercial Cost-Control Handbook*. Chicago: Crain Communications, 1972.

Brown, Les. *Television: The Business Behind the Box*. New York: Harcourt Brace Jovanovich, 1971.

Cohen, Dorothy. *Advertising*. New York: John Wiley & Sons, 1972.

Costa, Sylvia Allen. *How to Prepare a Production Budget for Film and Video Tape*. Blue Ridge Summit, Pa.: Tab Books, 1973.

Diamont, Lincoln, ed. *The Anatomy of a Television Commercial*. New York: Hastings House, 1970.

Heighton, E. J., and Cunningham, D. R. *Advertising in the Broadcast Media*. Belmont, Calif.: Wadsworth Publishing Co., 1976.

Hilliard, Robert L. *Writing for Television and Radio*. New York: Hastings House, 1972.

Mandell, Maurice I. *Advertising*. Englewood Cliffs, N.J.: Prentice-Hall, 1968.

Mayer, Martin. *About Television*. New York: Harper & Row, 1972.

McMahan, Harry Wayne. *How to Evaluate Your Own TV Commercial*. East Greenwich, R. I.: Weaver Publishing Co., 1973.

McNiven, Malcolm A., ed. *How Much to Spend for Advertising?* New York: Association of National Advertisers, 1969.

Roman, K., and Mass, J. *How to Advertise*. New York: St. Martin's Press, 1976.

Ross, Wallace A. *Best TV & Radio Commercials*. New York: Hastings House Publishers, 1968.

Sandage and Fryburger. *Advertising Theory & Practice*. Homewood, Ill.: Richard D. Irwin, 1975.

Seehafer and Laemmar. *Successful Radio & Television Advertising*. New York: McGraw-Hill, 1969.

Simon, Morton J. *The Law for Advertising and Marketing*. New York: W. W. Norton & Co., 1966.

Steiner, Gary. *The People Look at Television*. New York: Alfred A. Knopf, 1963.

Willing, Si. *How to Sell Radio Advertising*. Blue Ridge Summit, Pa.: Tab Books, 1970.

Wright, Winter, and Willis. *Advertising*. New York: McGraw-Hill, 1971.

Young, James Webb. *A Technique for Producing Ideas*. Chicago: Crain Communications, 1970.

Broadcast Bureaus

Television Bureau of Advertising, Inc.
1345 Avenue of the Americas, New York City, New York 10019

Radio Advertising Bureau, Inc.
555 Madison Avenue, New York City, New York 10022